GATEWAY TO HEAVEN

FIFTY YEARS OF LESBIAN AND GAY ORAL HISTORY

Clare Summerskill

Tollington

First published in 2012 by Tollington Press, London
www.tollingtonpress.co.uk

A catalogue record for this book is available from the British Library.

ISBN 978-0-9560173-7-6

Cover photograph of the entrance to The Gateways
by kind permission of Imogen Shepherd-DuBey

Cover design by jenksdesign@yahoo.co.uk
Typeset by Helen Sandler

Printed in Great Britain by the MPG Books Group, Bodmin and King's Lynn
Text pages printed on FSC-certified paper from well-managed forests
and other controlled sources

CONTENTS

CONTRIBUTORS

Barbara

Rex Batten

Linda Bellos

Kevin Boyle

Ian Burford

Peter Burton

Gill Butler

Alex Cannell

Bob Cant

Carl

Carol Chaplin

Emmanuel Cooper

Peggy Curtis

Cyril

Ros Dalgarno

Dan

Stephanie Dickinson

Taz Din

Val Dunn

Roger Fisher

Susan Hemmings

Bob Hodgson

Nick Hughes

Nic Humberstone

Colin Hutchens

Jack

Jimmy Jacques

Leonard Kemp

Bob Lewis

Mary McIntosh

Sharley McLean

Gerard McMullan

Norma

Ossie Osborne

Sarah

Sue O'Sullivan

Stanley Peters

Jenny Potter

Irene Sagar

Ron Strank

Gamal Turawa

Griff Vaughan Williams

Vito Ward

Jeffrey Weeks

Jean Winstone

Peter Y

INTRODUCTION

When people talk about their lives, people lie sometimes, forget a little, exaggerate, become confused, get things wrong. Yet they are revealing truths [...] the guiding principle could be that all autobiographical memory is true: it is up to the interpreter to discover in what sense, where, and for what purpose.[1]

Between 2004 and 2011, I interviewed forty-six older lesbians and gay men about their lives and experiences from the 1940s to the 1990s. They told me stories relating to personal, social and political history from the twentieth century. Historical documentation of many of the areas that this book covers is limited and as the people with memories of these times and events are now ageing, this relatively neglected area of history is at risk of going unrecorded.

Extracts from the interviews describe the contributors' experiences of living in a society where the majority of people's sexual orientation differed from their own. They recall a period in which lesbians and gay men were significantly more restrained both legally and socially than they are today. Not only have their voices been largely unheard but also, over their lifetimes, they may have had few opportunities to express their experiences in a non-threatening environment. Furthermore, the memories of gay men and lesbians who are working-class (a term with which some of the contributors are pleased to identify), without such mouthpieces as biographies or printed memoirs, are all the more likely to have gone unrecorded.

In the past I have written several plays and films from interviews with different groups in society, based around a specific theme or subject, some for the reminiscence theatre company Age Exchange, and several for my own theatre company, Artemis. Over two decades of gathering memories in this way and working with verbatim theatre (a form of theatre where there is nothing in the script that has not been said by one of the contributors), I have discovered many advantages, but also a few drawbacks, to recording history in this way. Oral history is, by its name and nature, passed on by word of mouth, and in the work I have done interviewing contributors, the facts they recount are usually not double-checked by the interviewee for accuracy. Before a play or a film is finally produced, important dates and historical information can be verified, but everything else told in the interview is from the contributor's own memory and viewpoint and is not altered without their suggestion or permission.

Partly for this reason, in some circles, oral history has not always been considered as reliable as other forms of historical documentation; but many existing historical records are also possibly inaccurate to a certain degree, by virtue of the subjectivity of those who recorded them. And if not inaccurate, then the material we read in standard history books might have other biases: history written by and about white men; or by and about heterosexual people; history of towns rather than of rural areas; a preponderance of books written about wars and political developments rather than social history; and so on. Until recent years it has been largely the hegemonic groups in society rather than those from marginalised communities who have recorded their own versions of past events. And as the historiographer Thomas Postlewait reminds us that: "History belongs to those in power."[2]

One of the greatest advantages to recording personal, social and political accounts of history from a contributor who has given their story during an interview is that we get to clearly hear their *voice*. They are not invited to offer a totally unbiased view. They know that they probably couldn't do that, even if they tried. They are asked for their personal opinion on a specific matter and their own recollections of that subject. They can speak their truths, tell their stories and even decide not to tell certain parts, revisit their histories in whatever way they choose. I have found that this freedom of expression allows their narrative to be vibrant, fun and moving in a way that conventional history books often fail to achieve. Partly for this reason, when I transcribe contributors' interviews I generally do not 'tidy up' sentence formation or grammar. Having worked with interviews for so many years now I find that when I read one through I can 'hear' more of that person's personal story if I leave in, rather than smooth out, their own distinct way of speaking, their dialect, their unique voice. Every now and then, when a contributor looks over an extract of their interview that I wish to use for a project, they tell me they would like certain colloquial phrases, repetitions or the odd bit of grammar amended, but I try to persuade them (up until now, successfully) to keep the words in just the way that they were first related.

Twenty-three of the contributors included in this book initially gave me their stories for a play that I wrote entirely from their memories in 2004, called *Gateway to Heaven*. Both the writing and the national theatre tour that followed were funded by the Arts Council.

I have taken the title of that show for this book. It refers to The Gateways, which was one of the most famous women's bars, located in Kings Road, London, and featured in the film, *The Killing of Sister George*; and Heaven, which opened as a gay men's nightclub in the 1980s and remains one of the largest and most popular gay dance venues in Europe.

After Age Concern (now Age UK) saw *Gateway to Heaven*, the play, they commissioned a film version which is still being shown around the country at LGBT film festivals and at events during LGBT History Month. A couple of years later, the Metropolitan Police saw it and, together with Age Concern Opening Doors, commissioned me to write a similar piece, based entirely on memories of older LGBT people about their relationships with the police over their lifetimes. The Criminal Justice Act 2003 had added sexual orientation to the list of aggravating factors in 'hate crimes'; and the Met were interested in examining why there was such a low level of reporting of homophobic hate crime from older people in London. For that project I interviewed a further twenty people and produced a film called *Queens' Evidence*.

Additionally, there are some interview extracts here from a 2011 theatre project I was involved in called *Staying Out Late*, which, through improvised scenes and a scripted performance, looked at older LGBT people's hopes and fears about care in later life, specifically with regard to their sexuality. These three projects are the main bodies of work that have provided me with the material that appears in this book.

Over the time that I have been working in the area of oral history, it has become an increasingly popular and accepted form of documentation. Several archives are now pleased to receive and record aspects of history in the form of interviews, both orally recorded and filmed. There has also been a general growth of interest in gathering memories from people from marginalised communities, which have included gay men and lesbians, and now several groups and archives hold collections of those interviews. I believe that there are two main differences between such collections and those presented in this book: firstly, the direct involvement that several of the contributors to this book have had in participating in and influencing areas of lesbian and gay history over the latter half of the last century; and secondly, I have chosen to arrange extracts under different chapter headings (rather than one complete interview after another) so that the reader is easily able to access stories about specific historical events, political and social groups, or personal testimonies. Additionally, I have written a personal introduction to each chapter to provide some historical context for the interviews and offer my own thoughts and analysis.

The large majority of contributors to this book were living in London and the South East of England when I interviewed them but many of them originally come from all over the United Kingdom as well as from countries such as Barbados, Germany, Tanzania, Thailand and the USA. Some of them played extremely important roles in lesbian and gay history, effecting political and legal change through their involvement in political groups, whilst others perhaps would not have seen their experiences as anything other than getting on with their lives, as lesbians and gay men, the best way they knew how.

Although the stories shared in this book cover a broad range of subjects spanning a period of six decades, there are some areas of lesbian and gay social and political history that were either not mentioned or only mentioned briefly by those whom I interviewed. Consequently there will be some pubs, clubs, groups, events and movements that are not referred to in this particular collection of memories.

Some of the contributors have told me they are happy for their full names to appear in print, while others prefer to use their forename only. For the sake of consistency, above each extract I have credited the contributor by their first name – a pair of names indicates a couple who were interviewed together. I am, of course, totally indebted to all of the contributors for their stories and I hope by reading them in this book that many more people will learn about our own often unrecorded – and at times, barely visible – social and political history. I have found the collecting and editing of these memories exciting, moving and important and I hope that you will too.

Clare Summerskill, London, 2012

1

GROWING UP GAY

At the start of each interview for the theatrical version of *Gateway to Heaven* I asked the same question: "When did you first realise that you were gay?" This generally led to the contributor telling me about their childhood and teenage years, the time when most of us gay folk realise, with no-one there to actually spell it out for us, that we are somehow different from the others. Ron describes his own experience of this: *"By and large you get the picture that your choices and interests are not really shared by the majority and you find yourself a little bit on the outside looking in."*

After realising that we are different, most of us will then try to seek out others who might be similar. This can be a difficult step but for some lesbians and gay men, especially those who are now of the older generation, it may have seemed, at times, an impossible one.

My first interviewee in this book, Cyril, says that he did not know he was 'gay' because he didn't know what the word was. Of course that in itself shows quite a significant difference between yesterday's and today's world – where there is now a word, or in fact several words, to describe the varying sexualities of human beings. The acronym we have reached as this book goes to print is LGBTQQI (lesbian, gay, bisexual, transgendered, queer, questioning and intersex, for those of you out of the loop). But in Cyril's childhood, not one of these terms was in common usage. In the mid twentieth century the terms used for men who loved men ranged from sodomite to invert, from pervert to pansy, names that you would undoubtedly not want to be called or to identify with. So, without names and without role models, gay men and lesbians had to somehow navigate their way through a growing awareness of their differing sexual orientation.

As part of my stand-up comedy routine I talk about how, when I say to people that I'm a lesbian, they sometimes say, "Yes, thank you very much, I don't want to hear about what you get up to in bed." To which I reply, "Well, I wasn't going to tell you!" The point behind this banter is that heterosexual people tend to immediately define lesbians and gay men by our sexual behaviour, even if we are not in a relationship or sexually involved with anyone. But, as any lesbian or gay person knows, there is much more to one's sexual orientation than who we are with (or not with) and much of it is first experienced and discovered in our teens, or even when we are pre-sexual. It might have manifested itself by simply adoring a teacher or an older girl (or boy) at school, but we knew that those feelings, however strong, were at the same time somehow forbidden, unaccepted, seen as different – and because of this, we learnt how to keep silent. We may have come out quite happily later in life, perhaps as a student or even much later, after a marriage, but in our childhood our initial instinct was to keep quiet about our newly discovered feelings, however joyful or exciting they may have felt.

CS

~

Interviews

CYRIL:
Well I didn't know I was gay because I didn't know what the word was then. But I do remember at the beginning of the war, about 1940 – so I would be about ten or eleven – my parents had a pub and they used to lodge soldiers and sailors, billet them on us. And I can remember going into the bathroom one

morning and there was this guy with his back to me and he was as brown as a berry and he was wearing dark trousers, must have been a naval guy I think, and I walked in and I was quite surprised and he turned round and he'd got lather on his face to shave. And of course that, against this wonderful smile he gave me! I remember being absolutely riveted and I didn't want to move but I knew I had to move and I'm sure I went absolutely red-faced and I sort of staggered out, but it has stayed with me ever since. I can always remember being really turned on by it.

Then the next time, I remember we moved from that particular pub to a much bigger one in Lancashire, in St Helens – that was in about 1942, so I would be about thirteen. There were outhouses in this place. We'd only been there a few weeks and I was pottering through rubbish in these various outhouses and I came across a book of photographs and they were of a German wrestler or boxer called Hackenschmidt. It was mainly in costume but in one of the photographs he was nude and I was absolutely mesmerised, just looking at it and closing it and then having another look, and being quite turned on. I knew it was wrong to be looking at it but I didn't know why and I put it away. A few days later I had to go back and have another look and finally my conscience got so bad I actually threw it away in the dustbin. I was so frightened.

I didn't know any gay people. I was aware, because other people had pointed them out, of the odd obviously gay guy, and in Lancashire they would say, "Oh, he's a right pansy," because they were limp-wristed guys really, and you'd think, "Oh I'm not like that."

SHARLEY:
I was born on 26 May 1923. Without knowing the word, I was probably aware of being gay as a young teenager. I can remember one of my girlfriends found a boyfriend and I just could not understand why she should prefer him to me, and that is going back a long, long time, but I wouldn't have labelled it 'gay' at the time.

CAROL:

When I was about eleven, I had lots and lots of girlfriends, and with one of them, I used to nip out at night and go across and sleep with her. But not like that. Nothing ever happened. But I was madly in love with her and I used to sleep next to her and think "Oh my God!" and I was sweating and I wanted to put my arms around her but you couldn't. So, eleven, I knew I was different from everybody else.

There was no-one like me that I knew, so when I got to reading some of the books at the library, I found myself and I started wearing my dad's clothes when he was out. Then I'd hide them in my bedroom and at night I used to put them on and go out walking when everyone was in bed. And of course no-one realised, they thought that I was a lad anyway, and it was fun because girls used to look at me and I'd think, "Ooh, if only I was a boy, wouldn't it be lovely?" That was what I wanted to be, I wanted to be a boy really. I think a lot of gay women have gone through that as well.

GERARD:

I was born in a part of Belfast that was almost totally Catholic, so it was like being in a little village even though you were in the city, because everyone in all the streets knew each other. We used to play games where we dressed up as Superman and Flash Gordon and we used old plastic macs and I enjoyed that. I always wanted to be Ming the Merciless in Flash Gordon. He was the baddie who had a great cloak but he was quite a camp person anyway... and of course then you could fancy Flash Gordon!

I suppose it must have been around twelve, thirteen, when hormones were beginning to kick in, that you first noticed anything. I can remember having a feeling when this boy grabbed my genitals and I thought, "Oh I quite like that!" And with the "I'll show you mine if you show me yours", it was almost a sense that that meant more to you than it did to them.

SARAH:

I remember when I was about four or five, I had this sort of scrapbook and on the cover I wrote, "My book of pretty laddies". I meant ladies, and I was fascinated by it and I've still got it.

When I was at school there was one teacher and I was absolutely mad about this woman – who was very beautiful, I must say – and all the other girls knew. I used to tremble when I saw her and then one day she asked me to come to London to a concert. Gerald Moore was playing the piano, and I met her in London and she took me in a taxi to a music club, somewhere near the Albert Hall, and she took my hand in the taxi and I was so flabbergasted that I immediately took it away. I thought it was all right for me to love her but certainly, when she got too close, I was terrified.

BOB C:

I was born in Scotland in Dundee in 1945 and I think it was when I was about fourteen that I realised that I might be attracted to other boys and I just found it unimaginable as to what this meant. I had a particular close friend who was very unlike me. He was captain of the football team, played football, played golf, all that sort of thing, and I didn't do any of those things at all. In retrospect I knew what I felt about this boy was desire and I suppose, really, that I was in love with him, but I couldn't have given it that name. The only names that were around were sort of fairly horrible really. There were words like 'queer', but there were local names as well. There was this man that used to sell bread and sandwiches at the school gate at break time and he was known as a 'sneck'. I think this is peculiar to the east of Scotland because I've never heard it since and it was said with such abuse, such contempt. There wasn't any suggestion of him being a paedophile or anything like that, he was just alleged to be interested in other men.

I remember going to a dance and I was kind of standing around on my own and this older man came up to me and started chatting away. I remember him saying he was getting so turned on watching the women dance so would I come into this side room with him? And because I was such a polite lad, I did. But then he suggested that maybe we should go and relieve ourselves in the public toilets. I was about eighteen then and I was just absolutely astonished, but I wasn't horrified.

JENNY:

I first fell in love with a woman when I was five. My mother was American and I was born in 1940, so this was just after the war, and we went over on a boat to see my grandmother who I'd never met. On the train down to the port was this gorgeous redhead with splendid tits and I just thought she was lovely. She was on the boat with us and yes, I thought she was marvellous. So my way of drawing attention to myself was to stand on her feet and punch her and she thought this was frightfully amusing. It took about three or four weeks to cross the Atlantic, or so it seemed at the time, and I was always buzzing round her. I always remembered her and years later I asked my mother, "Mum, do you remember a gorgeous redhead, quite well-endowed woman, who came over on the boat with us to America?"

"Yes," said my mother. "And furthermore, all the way down from Liverpool Street she held hands with an ATS woman." So obviously I picked it up pretty early on, I think.

I fooled about a bit at boarding school. I had the odd crush on the odd teacher and some of my contemporaries that I liked a lot. Matron Something-or-other took a shine to me, I don't know why. Not that I had a thing for her because she was hugely gross. Well, so was I, actually. But she knew that I liked to be on my own so she very sweetly put me in the only single room in the school, which I was allowed to keep all year. But I had to be in charge of some slightly younger girls, I would have been about fourteen at the time, and they all wanted to practise kissing in case they met a boy, so they practised on me. I didn't know what I was doing, hadn't a clue. I just did what felt right. It didn't go any further than kissing but it was ever so nice. Yeah. All right, that. I didn't fall in love with any of these little girls, no, no, although I fell passionately for some of the teachers, the younger, funnier ones. Not young like my age, because they were obviously older, but anything over about twenty-six to forty-six, I'd fall madly in love with, particularly if they made me laugh. But there wasn't anything I could do about it. I couldn't show it. I just used to try and make them laugh and then they'd like me and my company.

Up to the age of about thirteen I kind of assumed that mostly girls really liked girls but they had to *pretend* they really liked boys. So that's what I did and it was quite a shock to find out when I got to fourteen that girls actually *did* like boys. "Why would they want to be chased around and hit with sticks?" I thought, "This is just so peculiar. I'm on my own here but I cannot be the only one."

JACK:
I spent all of my life in the theatre in one way or another and the first production I did at school was *Midsummer Night's Dream*. My voice hadn't broken and I got the part of Titania, the Queen of the Fairies, which was great fun. It was 1949 and on the morning of the first performance I was in the first form and there was a boy in the third form called David and he'd been in plays before and he said, "We have a tradition at the school that the boys in the upper third can chose somebody from a lower class in the play." And I said, "What do you mean, 'choose'?" And he said, "Oh, well, you'll see." After the play we were back in the changing room, which was one of the dormitories, and he just came into the cubicle where we were all changing and said, "I'm now here to claim my reward." And he took me in his arms and he kissed me on the lips. Not a down-the-throat kiss or anything like that. I mean, I was about twelve, he must have been about fourteen and a half, fifteen, and it was the most extraordinary thing and it possibly sort of brought to life something which stayed with me for the rest of my life.

He became a kind of lover but not in any sense in a physical way. We never had sex. We were very close and intimate in that we sort of held hands occasionally and kissed, and on the day that he left school there was a service in the chapel and I was singing in the choir and it was that fantastic piece where they sing, "God be in my head and in my understanding" and I was in floods of tears. That summer I went to Falmouth on a day out on my own. I went to the cinema one afternoon and blow me, just before the main film started, he walked into the cinema with a girlfriend and I was absolutely and totally destroyed. So that was the first sort of experience of feeling gay.

SUSAN:

I've always liked girls more than boys. When I went to university I started to have quite close relationships with women and it joined up, looking backwards, with feelings I'd had for girls in the sixth form. I'd been very popular with the lesbian teachers at school but of course I didn't actually use the word lesbian, 'cos we'd be talking about the late Fifties, early Sixties. I knew that they were hyper-interested in me and that there was sexual tension and it was a way of getting attention and approval from them. I'd come from quite an unhappy family so I looked to my grammar school life for love and affection and approval. There was one particular teacher who, I suppose, when I went to school at eleven she must have been in her twenties, and she remained at the school till I left. She was always very, very fond of me. I went to school in the Medway towns, Chatham, quite an impoverished area, and she would bring me up to London where she lived with her parents at that time and take me to the theatre. When I was a kid I was quite sickly and I kept having to go into hospital then and she wrote to me every day in hospital and I kept those letters for ages. As I said, very unusual and very intense. She always used to choose me to go into the stock cupboard to do all the stock sorting out and I can remember the physical tension of it. But of course it was never expressed.

Another thing that happened was that there were dances every year. About a third of the staff were gay and the teachers

21

had to be asked by the girls as their partners and one teacher, she always used to be hinting around November time, "Don't forget to ask me." So she used to be my partner and we used to do ballroom dancing and I'd say to her, "Well, I'll be the boy," and she'd say, "That's fine with me."

RON:

At my school there was this football match between the staff and the pupils and there was this teacher who was really very nice and suddenly he was transformed – and I wasn't the only one standing on the side, looking at this bloke. He appeared in shorts and a T-shirt. Well, now a T-shirt is commonplace but then, oh my God! He had this chest and a wonderful build and we just... you know, mouths dropped. And I know damn well that he was quite aware of the response.

I don't think, growing up through my school years, there was any real sexual activity but you caught glimpses of yourself from other people. There was a guy who was a school friend of mine and we were chums, again no sexual traffic and nothing was actually said, but our interests and all that made us bond quite well. And at fourteen, of course we settled down to write our first novel, 'The House of the Nightingales' or 'Gilded Spendour', a simple little number about St Petersburg and all that! And it was these kinds of interests, writing, theatre, whatever, that made you realise that perhaps you were part of... a phrase I wouldn't have used at that time... 'a subgroup'.

It was the unspoken thing because I think by the time one was thirteen, fourteen, one was very aware that this was a no-no area, that it was just unacceptable, that it just wasn't done. First of all, sex wasn't spoken about in the family. That was for the bedroom. There was that kind of repressive thing but certainly there were expressions that one would pick up – "Well he's not the marrying kind" – and there were those coded things that children are really quite perceptive about. They may not understand the nuts and bolts about it but they know things. By and large you get the picture that your choices and interests are not really shared by the majority and that you find yourself a little bit on the outside looking in, like school sports. God, how I hated school sports, and most gay men seemed to, and I did everything to get out of them, like not playing very well. I mean, who wants to play football? Rather be doing reading or whatever.

VITO:

I think I always knew I was gay but I didn't have a name for it. I was born in the North East and the word 'lesbian' wasn't used in my social circle. I knew I was different. I remember playing all the games that you played with your school friends, pretending you were all the different stars from the films and the musicals, Howard Keel and people like that, and I just remember that it was always more suitable for me to play the man than the woman, and I rather frowned on the feminine side of things and yet I was attracted to the feminine. Barbara Stanwyck was my icon and I think that was because she had a lovely deep voice and she played strong women's roles.

COLIN:

I think I'd always identified as gay even if I didn't actually have a gay identity, if you see what I mean. I always felt I was a bit different. I think, looking back, that I first realised I might be gay as young as eight or nine. I think it was the fact that at one of the prep schools I went to I never wanted to play with the boys, I always used to play with the girls.

I went to an all-boys school and there was inevitably a lot of indulging. It depended on how mature the boys were but it started at quite an early age. It was absolutely rife. It was a fairly macho, masculine society, but in one house the housemaster adopted a fairly liberal view, just let it happen. He just saw it as a phase that boys went through, but other housemasters were perhaps less tolerant.

I was actually asked to leave school because of my activities.

Someone reported me and there was an inquiry amongst the boys and there was an acknowledgement that I was rather active and so I got hauled up before the housemaster and I was then asked to leave. I was actually leaving at the end of term anyway so I went about ten days early. That was a very traumatic experience because I didn't actually have sex after that for about seven or eight years.

MARY:

I went to a girls' grammar school in High Wycombe, very classic 1940s and '50s, and everyone had a crush on one or other of the teachers. A few had a crush on other girls, like the games captain, but nearly always it was teachers. It wasn't everyone but at least half the class could identify which was the teacher that they had a crush on. My crush was on the music teacher and she was gorgeous. She was also our form teacher so I got a photo of us all having a picnic. At the school picnic we had to decide which teachers to invite so our form always invited her. But at some point I started thinking that my crush was different from other people's and I wasn't sure why. I couldn't have identified why it was more significant. For one thing, a lot of the others told their mothers about their crushes but I never told mine. For some reason I thought it not advisable to tell my parents.

Most of my teachers at school were older single women and the theory about them was either that they'd sacrificed all for teaching or that they'd had a fiancé that'd died in the First World War – and this was quite implausible in the case of some of them who looked extremely dykey.

EMMANUEL:

I was born in a tiny coal-mining village in Derbyshire called Pilsley, which was near Chesterfield. Most of the family that I was born into were coal miners but my father kept a butcher's shop in the village and I had two brothers and two sisters, so there was a big family network within there. I guess from the earliest experiences as a child I knew I might be gay but obviously I couldn't put a name to it. I couldn't identify what it was but somehow I felt that I was different and I did notice that I was interested in boys more than girls. Gradually the idea formed that actually I did prefer the same sex, although that was very scary and very frightening. I kept thinking that that was what I prefer at the moment, but one day a switch will click and I'll prefer the opposite sex.

At school you'd do it in the changing room, usually in the boys' toilet, in one of the sit-downs. The community itself was largely a coal-mining community, but it was also a farming community and I was friendly with one of the farmer families and I did it with one of them. I think that he was possibly gay and I thought that he was very sexy, and we did it on top of a haystack. We did it in an outhouse, and we did it in their toilet. With a lot of the boys that I went with at school, it would often be me that initiated it and I liked that, and if they initiated it I really wasn't that bothered. Looking back of course it never occurred to me at the time that there were all these power plays and control within the dynamics of a relationship. But there was one boy at school who I really did find terribly sexy and attractive and he wasn't the best looking but I only had to touch him and he immediately got an erection and off we went.

ROGER:
I never had girlfriends, I didn't like them at all. I went to the church youth club on Tuesday evenings and they had dancing and I remember one girl would insist on sticking her leg between mine when we were dancing and I found that really quite offensive so I never learned to dance properly.

I must have been about fifteen and the vicar had a little curate house across the road from us. He had two sons and a daughter. The middle boy, Martin, because we were about the same age we became friends and we had quite a good relationship. He seduced me. Quite definite about that. He seduced me and it was mutual masturbation. But I never thought any more about it. As far as I was concerned, it was pleasant. His father was eventually made the vicar and he moved away and more or less walked out of my life. He is gay. He went into the church and he's one of these gay priests you hear about in the Anglican church, or was, he's retired now.

ROS:

When I lived in Coventry I had a boyfriend, that was for appearances' sake and it was my brother's friend, so he knew that my mother wouldn't allow me to do anything with him, but we went round together in a gang. And when I was about seventeen I had a girlfriend called Val, not a girlfriend, a friend, you know, called Val, and I was totally in love with her and I just wanted to be with her all the time and I thought, "Well, I don't like men." I liked boys, chatting to them, but I didn't want them to do anything with me sexually. But I would have been quite happy if Val would have attacked me in the bed!

The nearest I ever came to anything being gay was when I went to see films, like *The Loudest Whisper* with Audrey Hepburn and Shirley MacLaine. They were accused of being lesbians and I thought, "Yeah I can understand that," because I was in love with both of them. I used to fantasise about them. And there was another film called *The Fox*, I can't remember who was in that. So I think I knew then that I liked women totally and I've never had sex with a man in my life. Nothing with men, so really, yes, I knew that I was a lesbian then.

GAMAL:

I grew up in a community where sexuality, sexual orientation... the homophobia in the black community is horrendous, it's horrendous. I remember as a child watching Larry Grayson on *The Generation Game* with my mum and my sisters and we were watching it and luckily the lights were off. So we were sitting there and God knows where this question came from, but my sister turned round to my mum and said, "What if Gamal was gay?" And my mum said, "If he was, I'd shove a red hot poker right up his arse." And that sort of told me that you don't tell anybody this.

JEAN:
I thought that I might be gay from the time I started reading literature, which was about nine or ten. I knew that I felt more towards women than towards men and when I was a bit older, in my teens, I read *The Well of Loneliness*. I lived with my mother and my aunt, she read a lot of literature. My father was killed in the Second World War and my mother was bringing up four children on her own and there weren't many books around. But because my aunt was there, I was reading books in my teens which I wouldn't normally have had access to. Then I went to grammar school in Bristol. I happened to be very good at sport so, obviously, I was in love with my PE teacher, etc etc, and I was, at one time, going to talk to her, but I didn't.

I always knew the whole time that I was gay. During my teenage years I used to go out with my friends to coffee bars and reluctantly would be with a boy because my girlfriend wanted to be with another boy or whatever, 'cos you'd go around in groups like that. But in the sixth form I was actively looking but not saying anything, and then I went to a girls' PE college and I thought I was bound to find someone there. I was a very busy and active person, so I had a lot of social interaction with people, but I just never met a woman who I thought was gay. I'm a very physical person because I'm good at sport and I love women's bodies, and I used to look at paintings – and of course you'd read all the girls' books about girls going to boarding school together and I loved all that kind of thing. I was always looking for relationships between women.

REX:

I never ever thought of having a girlfriend and one of the things I'm absolutely certain of is that I knew I was gay from a very early age. It wasn't a case of being corrupted by anybody. I didn't really know what I wanted but I knew I wanted to find out what I wanted.

2

ONCE I HAD A SECRET LOVE

After the realisation that, as lesbians and gay men, we were somehow different from our peers – a discovery that often emerged during our teenage years in the form of strong feelings towards people of the same sex – we then had to seriously take stock of what might be happening and what we proposed to do (or not do) about it. That makes it sound as if we had some choice in the matter, but in reality, during those impressionable and formative years of our teens or our twenties, I am sure we often didn't think too much about it. Many of us just acted on it, as soon as we possibly could.

In retrospect, I feel that I was personally quite fortunate in not becoming aware of my sexual orientation until I went to university. I had the usual passionate crushes on teachers at school but although they were completely heart-rending and inevitably unreciprocated, my fantasies around these poor unsuspecting women were about caring and adoring and not actually of a sexual nature. If I had recognised the nature of my sexuality and had wanted to pursue my desires sexually in my teens, I might have ended up in all kinds of trouble at school and elsewhere. But I see myself as lucky that it was not until I became interested in the Gay Soc at my college that the penny dropped and I realised that I must be a lesbian. LGBT societies are now ubiquitous in colleges and universities, but for lesbians and gay men older than myself there was often nowhere to go to find out about other people like us: no books to look up at the library, no gay bookshops, no search engines on computers and no-one to help them around developing awareness and understanding of their own sexual orientation.

Gerard admits: *"I wanted to come to London because London meant to be unknown and to be able to have the opportunity to seek sex."* People who felt they might be different sexually from the majority had one thing they could do – move away from their home town to a larger city where their behaviour would at least be anonymous. This allowed them to seek out and explore their sexuality and not be labelled or vilified as 'the only gay in the village'. In his book *The World We Have Won*, Jeffrey Weeks creatively refers to such people as 'sexual migrants'.[1]

The periods that contributors talk about in this chapter range from the late 1930s, when Stanley's stories are set, to the 1960s, the era that Ozzie, Peter and Carol all describe. But right up to the present day, young people move to cities to enable them to explore their sexuality in a way that may not be possible in small towns or rural areas.

To some people, gay men and lesbians not only present a threat to heterosexual values and lifestyles but also challenge society's accepted gender stereotypes. I understand human sexual orientation as a spectrum, where some people are straight, some are totally gay or lesbian, some are drawn to those behaviours, and some cross genders or live in the space between. These days, transgender people may have surgery to physically transition to the gender that they feel themselves to be, but were not assigned on their birth certificate. Others, both gay and straight, identify as transvestites. However, Carol talks about a gay and lesbian community of cross-dressers in the Sixties who all lived around her in London. She tells us: *"In Earls Court we had a fantastic community of gays – gay men and gay women – and we all got on great and helped each other, and all the queens in Earls Court gave me all my drag."*

At that time lesbians were encouraged to define themselves as butch or femme and there was nothing in between. This meant that the 'butches' at the time had to completely take on the more masculine role. Carol says: *"You'd be laughed at if you wore women's knickers so you had to do the whole bloody thing."*

30

Whether such women were what we now understand to be transgender is a question that can probably not be answered because their behaviour was determined by the rules (albeit created by other lesbians) of the time, not applicable in the present. In today's society some lesbians can choose to either transition or to wear men's clothes and other lesbians will choose not to dress in that way, but there is a freedom of choice about these issues that did not exist in the period about which Carol talks. Because of this significant change we cannot know whether lesbians like Carol and her friends would have ever called themselves transgender, since that term did not exist and, as I suggest above, at the time their behaviour was often determined more by expectation than by choice.

So many stories in this book show us how some of the contributors struggled for a long time, often in torment, with accepting and acting upon their own sexual identity. One of the main reasons for such inner turmoil was not just that society was (and religious establishments were) highly condemnatory of non-heterosexuals, to the point of criminalising them, but also that there were no positive examples of lesbians and gay men to look to or to emulate.

A major difference nowadays is the presence of what might be termed 'gay and lesbian celebrities'. One of the first of these was Martina Navratilova. No lesbian over a certain age can deny the importance of both this woman's career and her personal courage. Before then we had not seen a famous woman in either sport or entertainment admit that she was a lesbian, although we had heard a few of them vehemently deny it (yes, Billie-Jean, that's you!). And the message that we received from famous people denying that they were gay in itself did a lot of damage to us. It was confirmation of our own fear that to admit our sexuality would probably result in a failed career and condemnation by family, friends, colleagues and society in general.

Celebrity lesbians and gay men are now more numerous; and whatever we think of the 'celebrity culture' in which we live, it is undeniable that famous people coming out publicly have, by their raised profile and status, helped individual LGBT people with any worries they might have had about their own sexuality. To see successful lesbians and gay men come out in public office, entertainment or sport normalises our own sexual orientation and behaviour. It may also move forward the public perception of homosexuality, as straight people become aware of the continuing and increasingly unashamed presence of LGBT people in our society.

CS

~

Interviews

CAROL:
In 1962, when I was seventeen, I came to London and I met some gay women who'd been in the army and I thought, "Wow, this is it now, I'm OK." They'd been thrown out of the army for being gay, typical, and put through shock treatment and God knows what and run away from the army. They were two very butch women in drag and another woman, Judy, she was in dresses. I really fancied Judy but she was with Sparky. But we used to get on very well and we all shared a flat and Smithy, the really butch one, fancied me. The thing was, I used to dress just casual like I do now, but in those days it was really butch or really femme and I didn't fit in.

If you went out anywhere there were women in suits and Brylcreem and women in dresses and ladies' things, and I didn't fit in to either thing so I had a lot of problems with women chatting me up and all that sort of stuff, butch women especially, and I didn't want it. So I thought the only way round this was... I'm going to have to do something. In Earls Court we had a fantastic community of gays – gay men and gay women – and we all got on great and helped each other, and all the queens in Earls Court gave me all my drag. They gave me shirts, suits, everything you needed. Not underwear, I got my own.

Had to get men's underwear as well because you were taking on the role, you had to do it properly, the big butch role. You'd be laughed at if you wore women's knickers so you had to do the whole bloody thing.

When I was living on my own, no way could I get accommodation in drag and there was no way I could change because that was my role then, my life, so I had to get girls, feminine girls, to get me flats. One flat I moved into in Kensington was... I mean all it basically was, was a room, a bathroom to be honest, and they'd put a board across the bath and that was your room. But I was so desperate to live somewhere.

I was only there a couple of nights and the landlord got to find out that I was in drag and he threw me out, physically threw me out. So it was difficult. But you see, you had to fit in, whether in the feminine role or the butch role – there was nowhere in the middle, you couldn't just be yourself, you had to act this role. A lot of women I knew who were in this butch role were actually quite femme and some of the femme women were quite butch, but you had to fit into one or the other. It was quite difficult really.

CYRIL:

I wanted to join an amateur theatre group so I spoke to somebody in the pub who said, "I'm a member of this one which is called the Phoenix. I'll introduce you." So I then met a man called Gordon and I suddenly began to think, "I wonder if Gordon's gay?" And one evening I went round to his house and we were just sitting there and I remember saying, "Gordon, can I ask you something?"

"Yes what?"

"Well, erm are you...? You don't mind me asking you this do you? Are you erm... are you gay?"

And he said, "Yes."

"Well, it's just that I think, I'm not saying I am, I think it's possible that I am too."

And he said, "Oh really?" With a twinkle in his eye. Then he said, "Look, I've got to go and make a phone call so if you don't mind I'll just slip out and if you'd like to look at these books while I'm away."

So off he went on his motorbike and I picked up his books and they were Tom of Finland and drawings. They were famous big butch guys in leathers with enormous, horse-like cocks. It was ridiculous! I was looking at these things and I realised, you know? It just knocked all the doors down. There were little pictures of guys being picked up and actually having sex and I thought: "Yes!" It was incredible. It was the first time I'd actually seen anything like that. I'd never read anything, any books and I just remember being left with these books and thinking, "This is what it's about. This is what I want."

Looking back now I realise that he was wonderful. He didn't have to go out and make a phone call, there were phones in the house. He just left me and then he came back and I just sort of said, "Gordon!"

And he said, more or less, "Welcome to the club."

Nothing happened with Gordon but he opened up the whole world for me basically and over the months we used to build sets and Gordon was very good at designing costumes. The Phoenix theatre company was a mixed club. The majority was straight but there was a nucleus of gay people and for the first time I could actually be myself and it was tremendous. It was wonderful.

ROGER:

It wasn't until I was twenty-two when I was, if you like, taken home by another male nurse, a senior on night duty, and I went to bed with him and he said, "You're a homosexual."

I said, "I'm not!"

"Oh yes you are. If you're not, why are you in bed with me?"

And I never looked back from then on.

We were on night duty. He was a German. Tall, slim, ten years older than me, so he'd have been thirty-something. He'd been in the German army on the Russian Front. After the war he came to Britain and did mental illness nursing, qualified and came to do general nursing and he was a senior student to me, as a junior. On the ward at night of course, you get periods when it's very quiet and at times as I'd go past he'd grope me. So it was a bit of a lark, you see? People do that sort of thing as a joke.

It must have gone on two or three times up and down the ward and this particular time, I just groped him back. So he said, "You can continue doing that." So I did. And it went on from there. We ended up in the sluice. He said, "Come back with me in the morning." So I did. But it just seemed like a normal progression. He had more qualms than me when we first met, but I never did. From that moment on, for me it was, "Oh I'm gay, that's it." But of course you had to be sensible and careful about it. That was part of life.

JACK:
In London when I was twenty I had my first physical experience with another man. I was picked up in a cinema and taken back to a flat in Earls Court Road and that was it. In the cinema he was sitting next to me and it was a sort of leg contact / arm contact – what I subsequently came to understand as being groped. Then a whispered message, "Shall we leave?" And I said, "Yes."

I knew what the codes were but what I did not know at the time, and what was terrifying and horrifying and also fantastic at the same time, was that walking back to his flat, I didn't know what was going to happen physically. The first thing that happened was that when he kissed me he forced my mouth open and his tongue went into my mouth and that was the first time that that had ever happened to me. There was a lot of sucking and licking and all of that. No penetration on this first occasion but it was sort of electric. Absolutely electric.

VITO:

I had my first relationship when I was twenty-one. I was in the Wrens when I met Sandy. She played in the same hockey team as me and her parents lived in Dorset and she invited me there for weekends and she obviously fancied me. We always slept in the same bed together and it happened in her parents' house and it just seemed the most natural thing in the world. I think I'd been building up to it for some time. We stayed together for some time, a couple of years. We thought we were the only ones, we didn't think there was anybody else like us at all.

I was away one weekend and when I got back I found that Sandy had been taken with some of the more well-known lesbians to a pub in Southampton. She was gob-smacked because the women there... I mean, it was a rough dive! It was near the docks. It was called The Horse and Groom, one of those pubs where anything went: prostitutes, guys from some of the smaller merchant ships, and some rough types, different ethnic groups, people who wouldn't normally be able to go into a British pub and have a decent drink, so they were all drawn to this pub. Sandy told me all about this, so of course I had to go.

The pub was a nice little bolthole for all the Wrens that were in the Portsmouth and Southampton area and when I went it was just mind-blowing. The women there were very stereotyped, very butch and very feminine. Even if a person wasn't feminine they had to be femme or butch. You couldn't be in between, you couldn't be yourself. Of course in a way we were emulating heterosexual relationships, I suppose. The butch females all wore suits and all had men's names like John and Paul, and they'd change their names frequently and decide they didn't like Paul or whatever, and they'd give us names. I can't remember what they called me but I didn't want it! They were puzzled by Sandy and me because we were both relatively butch in a boyish sense.

BOB C:

I think what really made me come to terms more with my sexuality was when I was living in Africa. I was there in East

Africa for two and a half years, doing VSO. I was teaching in a secondary school and I learned to speak Swahili. In retrospect I know that that's what a lot of British white young graduates do. They go to the other side of the world to have sex with men as a way of coming to terms, or not coming to terms, with their sexuality. But it was good that I could speak to my partners as well as having sex with them. There were several men that I saw frequently and had sex with but there's all kinds of issues there about power and so on, and a white man having sex with a black man in Africa is laden with all kinds of difficulties.

EMMANUEL:
There was a toilet in the village in the village green which no-one ever went in but I popped into it. In Chesterfield there was always interesting graffiti on the walls of the bus station so you knew that bus stations were cruisy in some way and occasionally you recognised people hanging about but at the same time there was an enormous fear because it was so illegal and so frowned on and yet at the same time so important.

At college, I shared a room with another student who I found very attractive. The first night I came back after the holiday, he'd been out, so he came in and I was pretending to be asleep because I didn't want to enter conversation or whatever, and he stood there and got undressed and I saw him standing there with no clothes on. I think it was the first time I'd seen him standing with no clothes on and I had a wet dream about him, which was wonderful, I'd never had a wet dream before. Then I started going out and cruising along the front and picking up men.

So I started to pick up men and mess around but I really wanted a relationship so when the course was over I moved to London to get a job. But I was desperately lonely. I didn't know a single person in the city but gradually things got better, through meeting people, usually picking them up, moving into networks, becoming gay really.

Like lots of gay men I used to look with great interest at

shopping catalogues and I used to fancy the men in them, which is almost universal. Many, many young men, being isolated, used to fantasise about them. There were magazines like *Health and Strength* and one looked at them rather covertly. But the first book that I read which really influenced me in terms of gay identity, which of course is a terribly sophisticated concept, was *Giovanni's Room* by [James] Baldwin and although I didn't agree with it, it was serious literature. When *Gay News* started to appear and one saw occasional copies, that was indicative of the growth of gay subculture. I remember early on thinking that there was a gay subculture in literature and of clubs and of venues and of ways of signalling to each other where to go and what to do, but sometimes one felt that one didn't know enough about it. Then other books came along. I think E.M. Forster's book *Maurice* was really very influential in describing very beautifully the relationship between working-class youths and upper-class men and the desire that that can encompass.

NORMA:
I first thought I might be gay in my early teens but I never did anything about it. I had a little fling with a woman in Barbados before I came to this country. I didn't really put a name to it, it just happened and carried on happening! It probably went on for a year. I never really talked to anyone about it back there, because the woman who I was with was married. Her husband was a seaman so he travelled a lot and I had a boyfriend who was also a seaman, so it was almost "Well it's something we're doing because they're away and we're sort of fulfilling each other's needs." But we never really discussed it.

I came to England in December 1960, just before my twenty-second birthday, but I didn't really understand anything about sexual identity. I had relationships with men and then had my children. I worked in a children's nursery and yes, I did fancy some of the staff there. I knew what it was called here but we had a different name for it back home, 'Wicca'. Someone would say, "Oh she's a Wicca." If you weren't interested in boys you'd get, "Oh, she's a Wicca," which means you fancied women. But I've heard it here because Sappho [the group] at one time was called Wicca Women or something like that and then they went back to Sappho.

I moved up to London in August 1967 and I got into a fling with a married woman. We lived in the same house. She was having problems and her husband slung her out because she was having affairs, so I put her up and we were having this conversation, talking about somebody else she knew, and I was lying there thinking, "Oh my God," and then I sort of reached out and cuddled her and she responded and she said, "I was dying to do that but I just didn't dare in case you were going to sling me out."

I think in the black community there are a lot of women who have relationships with women but have men in the background. They are married but everybody knows that they also have relationships with women. I suppose it's their way of surviving. They couldn't come out and have a full lesbian relationship. Even at home, when I think about it, in Barbados, there were a few women that people knew of in the neighbourhood. "That one's a Wicca." Because they were seen as very masculine women. But there were quite a few that you suspected but they weren't out in the open, they were probably married or had relationships with men as well.

GERARD:

I left school at fifteen and went to work in a department store in Belfast. I worked in the Gents' Ready Mades, we called it RM. In the Gents' Ready Made Department there was about a staff of five and I used to get on well with them. Looking back, two of the men were obviously gay, one of whom was a bit of a screamer. But I just didn't realise, because you had no experience, nothing for judging what this meant.

I wanted to come to London because London meant to be unknown and to be able to have the opportunity to seek sex. I can remember getting a *Gay Times* in London and then when

I'd read it in my flat, taking it out and putting it in a dustbin in the street because I didn't want to put it into my own dustbin. So that was the sense of the oppression one had.

I read a complaint in *Time Out* by someone saying that he and his wife were in London and they'd seen a film in this cinema and he said he couldn't hear for the noise of seats banging up as men walked around the cinema. So I naturally took a quick note of the cinema, which turned out to be one called The Biograph at the back of Victoria Station. I went along one Saturday evening to find it jam-packed, so packed that we were standing when I got in. You had to stand along the wall. But I realised that this was a place that other gay men came to, so although nothing happened on that first time, I knew this was somewhere to come back to.

I did go back to it and then realised the whole sort of rationale, which was that it put on any old movie that it could get and it ran them almost continuously. It had a central aisle and the left-hand side of the cinema was where gay men came and sat and went to make contact; and the right-hand side was where dossers came and sat to sleep in somewhere warm. So if you wanted sex you came and sat on the left-hand side. And the reason for the banging up of the seats was you sat beside someone and saw whether you were able to get on, whether anything would happen, and if anything didn't, you then had to move your seat. Well, the only way to do it was to get up, pretend to go the loo, and of course there were also things happening in the loo, and then come back and sit in a different seat where you could sit beside somebody else and start again.

So sex went on in the stalls and occasionally one might meet somebody who said, "Would you like to come back to my place?" That was something that did happen a couple of times to me. It was an opportunity to meet people in an environment, and also I liked the cinema and you were somewhere reasonably warm – and if you didn't manage to meet anyone, the cinema was going on. Sod's law was that if there was ever a film that was interesting, that was the evening that you actually got on with someone and if there wasn't anything interesting, that was the evening that you didn't meet anyone at all so you had to sit and watch the film. I have strange memories of an old Marlon Brando film which I sat through one afternoon and I didn't manage to get a grope with anybody and I took very much against Marlon Brando after that.

OSSIE:

In 1961, when I was twenty-nine, I went to work for the Government Car Service. It was a van service at first and then I went onto the cars but it was the van service where all the gays were. The whole garage, which was in Lambeth by the Thames, was gay, so we all had a wonderful time. When I walked into the garage for the first time, I couldn't believe it. The girls were coming in looking like men, going in the ladies' toilet, getting the skirts on and coming out like women, and I couldn't believe it!

This particular girl told me all about it and it all fell into place. We were going down to Hinchley Wood. We had a drop there and we were going through these woods and she said, "Look it's the woods, the woods!" and I said, "Oh, it's no good, bread and bread." 'Cos my mother used to say that, "bread and bread," meaning two men or two women, it's a saying. I knew that there was men but I didn't know about women at all.

Then we were going past the car service garage, which was in Kensington at the time, and she said, "That's known as the Lesbian Embassy."

So I said, "What does that mean?"

"Oh," she said, "you say some funny things."

She was telling me how the car service place was called the Lesbian Embassy. And, as I say, it all fell into place and I thought, "Well I've come home!"

STANLEY:

I grew up in the Cotswolds, the most beautiful place in the world, and I fell in love disastrously when I was seventeen. In about 1937 I saw an advertisement in the *Daily Telegraph* for a decorator who wanted to take a pupil, and I thought, "That's for me." So I wrote and got an interview. It was in Leamington Spa so I went up there and in the middle of the interview he suddenly kissed me! It was a tremendous shock but I found it very attractive. His name was James and he grabbed me and it was all rather exciting. So then unfortunately I fell in love with him which was a disaster because he wasn't really interested, he just thought it was rather fun.

I also went round the country outside, because there were masses of lorry drivers and you could pick them up at the service stations. Oh yes, it's well known, and thousands of them have got wives and children at home but they had a little bit on the side. Of course, you have to remember that quite a lot of people are impressed if you've got an upper-class voice, so it's quite easy to chat people up.

When I was living in South London, two or three lorry drivers used to spend the night, bringing their lorries outside at the place where I was living, spend the night and go home to their wives. Quite extraordinary. And if you'd ever said to them, "Are you gay?", they would have thumped you. But as long as you're charming and nice, they're quite happy. Of course there are frightfully aggressive people out there, but I know who not to look at. The sort that would go, "What are you looking at?" *Bang!*

One night I took two... never have two people... I took them home from Dorothy's Club in Knightsbridge. Oh yes, that was a mistake. I was rather drunk and I was at this club in Knightsbridge and they said, "Oh we'll take you back."

So they took me back to Chenies Walk and they separated in the drawing room, which was fifty-five feet long, huge room, and I was in one end talking to one and I thought he'd gone to the kitchen. I walked round the flat and found that he was in my mother's bedroom going through her dressing table.

So I said, "What are you looking for there? I think you'd better come into the drawing room."

So he came in – and she never woke up – and he must have gone to the kitchen and got a dreadful knife and he grabbed me and stuck this knife against my throat and I managed to say, "If you're going to cut my throat, there's a beautiful Georgian one in the drawer next door. I don't want my throat cut with that rusty old kitchen knife."

And he threw it on the floor and said to the other one, "Oh come on, let's fuck off." So they ran and I rang the police and they came round.

PETER B:
I think people always say that gay life has this thing where you transcend class barriers, which is absolute bollocks. If you're from the East End and you meet an aristocrat, you're still the East End bit of trade and the aristocrat's still the person paying. However, if you know what you're about, you work on what your potential is. You think, "I might be quite cute now but this won't last forever."

What I liked was meeting really interesting older people who'd say, "Must you read this rubbish? Read Isherwood, read Samuel Butler." They would take me to the theatre – and not just to see Irene Handl in *Goodnight Mrs Puffin* – and being a very young gay man on that West End scene and meeting people and knowing when not to speak and when to flutter my eyelashes and whatever, I got a fabulous education. I can remember when I was fifteen and someone first played me Lotte Lenya – and I've played Lotte Lenya for loads of people now and they've gone away and said, "Fabulous."

I'd left this awful school in 1960, but I'd always read and I think I'd always known from a very early age that out there was something better, and I worked out how to get it – and that's the thing that you can do in the gay world, or could then.

JENNY:
My first lesbian experience didn't occur until I was about nineteen when I was away working in Switzerland as a photographic technician and one of the girls working in this

photography shop and I just seemed to gel. We played this really stupid game of flicking rubber bands across the room and somehow we ended up in bed because a rubber band passed my ear, and the room I was in was so small that I was actually sitting on the bed, so she had to get past me to retrieve it and we found ourselves making love. It was absolute heaven and I've never forgotten it.

We had a wonderful winter of non-stop roly-poly. She was actually German and lived in Bavaria and after we'd spent that winter together in Switzerland, I decided to go and see her and stayed for about three months. Because she had this yearly and well-paid winter job in the Swiss firm, we could afford to take a couple of months off in the summer, so we just used to sort of bum around. She had a Vespa so we used to scoot all over Europe. We had a lovely time staying in peasant shacks and things like that. At hotels we'd say, "No, we don't mind a double bed. Don't worry, that's absolutely fine." Thinking, "Shit," if they gave us two singles. Once we went to stay somewhere quaint and quiet and we had this lovely double bed, what bliss! Then the innkeeper said, "We're a little over-booked tonight, this other girl's going to come and sleep on that mattress over there, do you mind? Terribly sorry." We minded very much, but there was nothing we could do about it.

Of course none of her friends knew and none of her family knew and my parents didn't approve anyway because she was a German and the parents were in the war so "What the hell was I doing anyway?" But I think they'd rather given up on me by that point. I'd already started working as a photographer's assistant in London so at least they couldn't complain about me frittering my life away. But in between jobs I would take some time off and go and see my chum. Our affair continued for about two or three years.

CAROL:
Tattoos were the thing to do because all the butch women had tattoos. They had a little cross on your hand between the

thumb and the first finger, everyone had a little cross. One of the girls did that to me, and that was my very first. And my friend Judy said, "You've got to have some more," and it was very painful. You did it with Indian ink and a needle. You sterilised the needle with a lighted match or something like that and you just tattooed the shape, or the sign. So then I got these, Judy did them. That's "True love", for Mum, that's a heart shape there and then she started on this one, "Mum", and I finished it myself. But the Indian ink fades out over the years. That was an Egyptian eye that I quite liked and that's two hearts with nothing in. At the time it was the fashion. It was the pressure to prove your butchness, you had a tattoo.

ALEX & IAN:

Alex: So I then met Ian, and I was of a Scottish Presbyterian background, so I was very cagey, particularly if anyone was English – I was very Scottish. I was sitting minding my own business one night in this restaurant and Ian came along and he said, "Is anyone sitting here?" And I said, "No." He said, "Would you mind if I joined you?" And I said, "Please do."

He did, and we fell into conversation and it's been going on ever since. We talked all night and it wasn't until the early hours of the morning that eventually there was a finger laid upon me! But it needed that sort of gentle approach to allow me to give freedom to who I really was as a human being.

Ian: When I met Alex I was acting in a show called *Pickwick*, which was quite a long run, and between shows we used to eat in what we used to call Posh Valottes and a lot of my friends were in *The Sound of Music* and we often used to meet in there between shows. We had the same matinees and we always used to go swimming at the Oasis. I went in this particular day and spotted this rather handsome lad sitting at a table all on his own, so I said with a slightly loud voice, "I'm just going for a quick swim, I won't be long."

So I whizzed up and when I came back again he was still

there. So I thought, "That's a good sign." I went over and I said, "Anybody sitting here?" You know, the old line, and he said, "No," very quietly, and so I said, "Do you mind if I join you?" So we started to chat and in the course of the conversation I said, "Have you seen the play across the road? I happen to be in it." So he came to see the show and he paid for his ticket too, so I thought that was a good sign. Then we met up afterwards. He came round and we went for a drink and then we came back to my place for a coffee and he stayed the night.

In retrospect I realise what enormous steps these were for him. Much less so for me because I was a little more practised in the art of seduction than he was. But he came and he stayed and we've been together ever since.

Alex: Suddenly there was a sort of frisson and I knew in my heart of hearts that this was my journey's end and it so happened that it was my relationship that's lasted forty years. I was twenty-three then.

Ian: We were the very first couple to register our partnership with Ken Livingstone's partnership register for the Greater London Authority. Zero zero one.

3

BEING ILLEGAL:
GAY MEN AND THE LAW IN THE 1950s AND '60s

This chapter looks at people's experiences and reflections about homosexuality and the law over two crucially significant decades, the 1950s and '60s. During this period gay men were being ruthlessly tracked down, entrapped and often charged with criminal offences. In the autumn of 1953, British gay men were the victims of what they termed 'The Great Purge' – a massive police crackdown on homosexuals in which nearly five thousand men were arrested on charges either of 'gross indecency' (the same law under which Oscar Wilde was imprisoned), solicitation, or sodomy. This represented an increase of 850% over the arrest rate for homosexuality in 1938, just before the Second World War.[1]

One of the contributors to this book, and specifically to this chapter, is Rex, who published an account of his own experiences and that of his friends during this terrifying time. Rex's book is called *Rid England of this Plague*.[2] The title comes from a declaration made by Sir David Maxwell Fyfe (the then Home Secretary) who, in the Fifties, was determined to clamp down on homosexuals. Rex mentions that during one of these purges, he was interviewed by the police about a man he had once known, and encouraged to turn Queen's Evidence (when a suspect provides information to help catch others). This was a method employed frequently against homosexuals by the police to enable them to widen their net and secure further arrests. This proposal was also made to another contributor, Jimmy, who talks in Chapter Nine about his experiences of being arrested.

While I stated in my Introduction that not all history revolves around politics and laws, during the 1950s and '60s substantial advances were made concerning the rights of gay men (and indirectly, those of lesbians) as the outcome of three important historical and political events. The first was the renowned Montagu–Wildeblood case of 1954. Lord Montagu, then a twenty-eight-year-old socialite and the youngest peer in the House of Lords, was one of three men convicted of 'consensual homosexual offences'. In a sensational week-long court case, he was tried together with his cousin, Michael Pitt-Rivers, and Peter Wildeblood, the thirty-one-year-old diplomatic correspondent of the *Daily Mail*. All three defendants were convicted. Pitt-Rivers and Wildeblood were sentenced to eighteen months in prison, and Lord Montagu was given a year's imprisonment.

But the prosecution provoked a wave of sympathy from the press and the public, many of whom felt that this case amounted to little more than an unedifying witch-hunt. The discussion that took place in newspapers and in people's homes, instead of merely sensationalising homosexual behaviour, served to highlight the fact that by this time the public did not appear to be so concerned as they once had been about the sexual behavior of consenting homosexuals. Emmanuel makes an interesting point about the impact of this particular court case by saying:

"I think with the Montagu case, it really caught the imagination of the nation in a very prurient way. The court case totally performed this conflicting role. It broadcast that it existed and that there was a network and people did it and desired it; and at the same time it made you into a criminal."

In the wake of the harsh prosecutions that followed this case and the public's reaction to the severity of the penalties inflicted on the men involved, the Wolfenden Committee was set up to examine the existing laws around homosexuality in Britain and also to rid the streets of overt displays of prostitution. From 1954 to 1957, the committee (comprising John Wolfenden CBE, three women and eleven other men) took evidence from police, prison officials, prostitutes, psychiatrists, theologians and others with supposed expertise. They also heard the evidence of homosexual men, who had to conduct their sex lives in secrecy, subject often to blackmail, and treated abominably when imprisoned for their 'crimes'.

The Wolfenden Committee deliberated for three years, meeting in private on sixty-two days. Concerned about the sensibilities of the secretarial staff dealing with the material, in internal memoranda they referred to homosexuals as 'huntleys' and prostitutes as 'palmers' – Huntley and Palmers being well-known biscuit-makers.

The committee's report, published on 4 September 1957, recommended that homosexual acts between consenting adults in private be decriminalised for those over the age of twenty-one. The press was, for the most part, outraged. Lord Rothermere's *Daily Mail* called it "legalised degradation", and commented, "Great nations have fallen and empires decayed because corruption became socially acceptable."[3]

The proposals were finally made law in the Sexual Offences Act of 1967, which was a milestone in terms of moving forward the gay rights agenda in this country. But not every gay man at the time was as pleased as the government perhaps thought they might be, on account of the legal restrictions that still determined homosexual behaviour – one of which being that it applied only to England and Wales, excluding Northern Ireland and Scotland. Ron describes the bill as *"an olive branch"*, but Rex asked, *"Where the hell have we got?"* and says, *"I wasn't that excited because, no, I didn't feel we'd moved into a new world at all."*

The ages of the contributors in this book vary and on certain subjects their opinions might reflect that age difference. Peter (Burton), who was out in his late teens in London, has a slightly different perspective of what the 1967 law meant to him as such a young man. He says: *"We weren't aware at that sort of age of the law itself. We weren't aware of the dangers from entrapment, blackmail [...] and in the West End there were quite a few young people about who were just carrying on regardless."*

In the 1960s, gay men still used their own secret language,

Polari, amongst themselves. This wasn't mentioned by any of the other contributors, but when I interviewed Peter for the play version of *Gateway to Heaven*, he kindly gave me a copy of his book *Parallel Lives* with the following explanations:

> "In the bar we'd stand round polarying with our *sisters, varda* (look at) the bona *cartes* (male genitals) on the *butch homme* […] If we had enough bona *measures* (money) we might buy a handful of *doobs* to *zhoosh* (throw) down our *screeches* (mouth or throat) – enabling us to get *blocked* out of our minds."[4]

As the social historian Stephen Pugh points out: "Polari [enabled] gay men to talk to each other without discovery, for who would risk telling the police that two men were conversing in Polari without disclosing their own secret?"[5]

The laws before and after 1967 did not, of course, affect lesbians in the way that they impacted upon and criminalised gay men's behaviour and general outlook. In 1921 the House of Lords had refused to make lesbianism illegal because they thought that if it was made visible it might encourage other women to become lesbians. The Speaker of the House had declared: "You are going to tell the whole world that there is such an offence, to bring it to the notice of women who might never heard of it, never dreamt of it. I think it is a very great mischief."[6] But whilst lesbianism in the UK has not been directly criminalised, there is an argument that legislation has been indirectly used to exercise judicial and societal disapproval of lesbians. Some would contest that laws relating to censorship, child custody, libel and slander, obscenity and sexual offences have featured in covert discrimination against lesbians.[7]

So, even though lesbianism has, over the last few centuries, been regarded as socially and even morally unacceptable, lesbians were rarely prosecuted for their sexual activities. It is clear that lesbians and gay men, although politically united now (on a good day, at least) in the general cause of securing increased social freedom and extended legal rights, have in some ways come to this point in the present via different routes, through differing historical and social events and perspectives. But it is always understood that the criminalisation of gay men's sexual activities has made an indelible mark upon not only their behaviour but also upon their general outlook, in both the past and in the present.

CS

~

Interviews

REX:
It was in the Fifties that the Home Secretary, David Maxwell Fyfe, famously claimed, "We will rid England of the plague of homosexuality," and he had a bloody good try! He said, "Look, the thing holding this country back are these queers and we must do something," which basically gave the police and the media *carte blanche* to do whatever they wanted, to arrest them as much as they wanted, harass them as much as they liked – and as far as the press was concerned, they were to publicise everything.

There was a guy I met when I was nineteen, who lived near Dorchester. I'd known him for three years and through him I'd met my lifelong partner and we came to London, this was 1951. But when I was twenty-three, this guy I knew was arrested. It was at that period, just after the Montagu case, and the police, well, they only had to ask around and they'd get my name attached to his. That was the problem in the Fifties. I was in London at the time and one morning I had a letter from my mother saying the police had been there the previous day and they wanted my address and she said, "How do you know my son's mixed up in this business?" And they said, "We have our ways of finding out." And she said, "Well, use your ways to find out where he is. Good morning." That was almost a tigress defending her cubs, wasn't it?

We were in a bedsitter in Camden Town and we came

home from work, my partner and I, and the landlady said the police had been here from Dorset today and that they were coming back at seven o'clock and it was obvious why they were coming back. What we did agree then was that we would admit nothing. So they did come back at exactly seven o'clock. They interviewed me in the flat and my partner in the police car outside.

I denied knowing the man they mentioned was homosexual. I don't even know if they used the word homosexual, they probably said pervert, I'm not sure. One of the things that did occur to me during this interrogation was that it was a little like a film script. I had had bit parts in quite a few of the old B movies, because you'd get three pounds a day, and that was almost a week's wages for some people, and in the films you had the friendly copper and the other one, the unfriendly one. Good cop / bad cop. And during the interrogation, what did occur to me was that it was like writing a film script – which of course made it quite a bit easier to me to stick to lying. But they must have known I was lying. And obviously in the bedsitter we had two single beds but one of them said, "You can get two in a bed, one on top of another if you want to."

They did ask – well, they did this in a lot of cases – would we turn Queen's Evidence? Well, I pretended that I didn't even know what they were talking about. The main thing they said was, would I go into court and tell the truth and their lawyers would help me? Whatever that meant. But I just claimed that I did not know what he was talking about.

Did they believe me? I'm sure they didn't. It must have been bloody obvious that I was lying. But I was talking to a lawyer friend of ours, well, only three or four years ago, about it, and I told her the whole story and she said, "Well, don't you see that you probably didn't fit the stereotype?" Because the police found I actually smoked a pipe and they persuaded me to smoke it, fill it and smoke it. Well, of course there were queer bars at the time, there weren't gay bars, but if you went into a queer bar sometimes you couldn't see across the bloody place for smoke, but if I lit up my pipe I'd get, "Put that stinking thing out!" You know? Gay men did not smoke pipes! They smoked cigarettes, but I smoked a pipe. In fact I started quite young because the village doctor smoked a pipe, so I was just copying him.

They eventually packed up and went away and never came back. Why? We never knew. We never dared ask. The whole thing worried us because my partner had a good job, doing well, but he would have lost it and no-one would have employed him again. I was twenty-three when that all happened. It was terrifying, not only for us, but it could have destroyed our families. In spite of everything, we came through and our partnership strengthened and lasted for forty-five years until his death.

RON & ROGER:

Ron: People of our generation were so conditioned about not writing notes. Whole groups of people could be condemned if they had a diary when the police picked them up. They were knocking on doors. You knew you could bring your friends down and everybody.

Roger: If you were wise you wouldn't write anything in a diary and I've never written a love letter in my life.

IAN:

We were in a sense a secret society up to a point, until we were legal in the Sixties, until you could do it in private without being imprisoned. On the other hand, it certainly didn't inhibit me, but it was undercover. There was always of course that element of danger in the sense that if you had a job other than an actor... but certainly in acting nobody gave much of a bugger about it. It was almost expected, you know? "All those actors, they're all poofs." But, on the other hand, if you'd been in any of the respectable professions, lawyer, politician, bank manager, you were open to blackmail. One heard of incidents...

The Montagu Case

JEFFREY:

The Montagu–Wildeblood case was about Lord Montagu, the founder of the motor museum, and Peter Wildeblood, who was the diplomatic editor of the *Daily Mail*. Wildeblood and a chap called Michael Pitt-Rivers were staying in a cottage on the south coast when they picked up two airmen who were then invited to Cliveden to a party, and Cliveden was of course the home of the Astors, and famous as a haunt of aristocratic laxness. But the airmen got back late to camp and were interrogated and eventually turned Queen's Evidence against Montagu, Pitt-Rivers and Wildeblood. Wildeblood was the only one who pleaded guilty but they were all convicted.

ROGER:

In the course of the questioning [of the airmen], the name of Lord Montagu turned up, so of course they probed deeper and then the civil police became involved. And the mire hit the fan, because it became clear that they had been to a party at which homosexual activities had taken place and a lord was involved, who was obviously a homosexual. Of course it was a *cause célèbre* at the time and in fact, because the public didn't go along with the media, screaming their breasts off as usual, as a result of that, it was the first step towards changing the law.

There was a chap called Peter Wildeblood who was the only one who not only pleaded guilty but said, "Yes, I am homosexual and I was doing this," and he went to prison for, I think it was something like a year or two years.

STANLEY:

I had a friend, Michael Pitt-Rivers, who'd been to prison along with Lord Montagu. They had a party at Edward's house in the country, Beaulieu Palace. They were great friends of mine and it was the fact that they went to prison that changed the law, because they said it was ridiculous that there was a law against men but not against women.

RON:
One thing the Montagu case pointed out was that Britain at that time was very buttoned up, very class-ridden, and the public may not have cared for our lifestyle but I do believe, certainly then, that they cared even less for injustice. They saw this group, whatever they were doing, and they were emotionally strong enough to say, "Well what people do in their private life... in their own homes... this is just dirt," and that led to a beginning of the change in the law.

REX:
In the early Fifties there were several high-profile cases where the police actively enforced laws prohibiting sexual behaviour between men. The best-known one was Lord Montagu. During the Montagu case I wouldn't buy or read any of the newspapers with the case in because I actually knew Michael Pitt-Rivers, who was Lord Montagu's cousin, who was in the case, and we were terrified that we might be dragged in there because I knew Michael Pitt-Rivers had my name and address in his address book.

EMMANUEL:
There was the Montagu case in 1953/4 which was splashed all over the papers in extraordinary detail for the time. Well, it was still a totally taboo subject and I just got so excited by this, not only wanting to go and be molested by Lord Montagu and Peter Wildeblood and thinking how wonderful and thrilling and exciting this would be... reading every word of it and realising through that that there were other people in the world who were like that.

I would have been about fourteen or fifteen then. We took

two papers, the *Daily Mirror* and the *Daily Herald* and then on Sundays we took the *News of the World*, which in those days was a broadsheet and was more serious and had enormous great reports from these trials and I just found it really quite extraordinary. But at the same time feeling terrible guilt so that whenever I went with one of the boys I always thought, "I'll never do it again."

I think with the Montagu case it really caught the imagination of the nation in a very prurient way. For most of the nation it would have reinforced their ideas that this is what these ghastly gay men did, you know? They molested young men and inflicted their will upon them and were devious and slimy. Whereas for gay men, they thought it was all terribly interesting. So the court case totally performed this conflicting role. It broadcast that it existed and that there was a network and people did it and desired it and at the same time it made you into a criminal.

Wolfenden Report

REX:
When the Wolfenden Committee was set up I know both of us, my partner and I, thought, well, forget it! There's no point in talking about it. It's set up to consider the evils of homosexuality and prostitution – so we were just lumped together, much the same as prostitutes – so there's no point.

RON:
Around the time of the Wolfenden Report, what was running at this time was a sea change politically and emotionally. We made an appointment to see our Conservative MP for Ilford, because at that time the bill was going through, the Wolfenden Report, covering sexual offences and whatever, and we said, "We've got to support this." So we went to see the MP, knowing full well that the committee members were a dodgy group. Ironmonger,

our MP was called. The only thing I can say about him was that he was an honest man. We said, "Will you support this bill?" Now we didn't spell it out that we were gay but why would we be there if we weren't?

And he said, "I've been in Parliament eleven years and I quite like it here, thank you very much. If you can guarantee me that I'll still be here if I vote for this bill, I'll vote for it." More or less meaning: "I'm not going to vote for anything that's going to change that."

Now we didn't like his answer but we admired his honesty. We sat in the public gallery for the debate and we never heard such witchcraft, such rubbish, and we heard such terrible, terrible prejudice.

So you were treading carefully, aware that there was change coming, but we were never sure when the law would change. When it did come, it said that you had to be twenty-one and only two guys were allowed in the house. If there was a third guy in the house and you were having sex and he wasn't involved, that was still illegal. All this rubbish, but nevertheless it was an olive branch.

1967 Sexual Offences Act

REX:
Gradually the change finally happened. I remember exactly where I was when the law was passed and it hit the local papers. I was on a bus passing the Old Vic Theatre and the guy next to me, next seat over, opened his newspaper and it said, "Homosexuality no longer illegal between two males in private." And the "in private" bit was, well a hotel was not private and I suppose if you were in a wood or anything like that, that was not private, and that was enforced. So I thought, "Where the hell have we got?" You had to be over twenty-one. Well, in fact I was sixteen when I knew what I wanted and I was certainly nineteen when I met a certain guy in Dorset, so even after the '67 act, that would have all been very illegal. So

I wasn't that excited because no, I didn't feel we'd moved into a new world at all.

But I do remember that one Saturday morning, not long after the act came in, my partner said, "Let's go out and buy a double bed." A double bed! And that was a hell of a statement to make because everybody in the street would know these two men had a double bed. We bought it in Peckham. Back then Peckham had several big department stores and nobody asked who we were and there were never ever any snidey remarks or anything in the street, we were just accepted as a couple and we never had any problem at all.

PETER B:

I left school at fifteen, 1960, and I knew what I was looking for and it was easy enough in London to actually encounter other men. It was seven years before the act when the law changed and I think a lot of people, certainly, growing up in a metropolis, didn't realise that as young teenagers what we were doing was against the law. So we didn't carry on as if we were against the law, which is why I think the change in the law was a historical inevitability eventually, because people of that sort of generation were not going to conform to the dictates of government. We weren't aware at that sort of age of the law itself. We weren't aware of the dangers from entrapment, blackmail, etc, etc, and in the West End there were quite a few young people about who were just carrying on regardless.

JEFFREY:

In 1967 I was obviously relieved that the law had been liberalised to some degree but remember it was a fairly restrictive change in the law. It wasn't legalisation of homosexuality, it was decriminalisation in private between consenting adults, over twenty-one, if you weren't in the armed forces or the merchant navy. So it was very limited and therefore I was pleased that it passed and followed debates in the press and on the radio, but it didn't feel as if anything remarkable had yet happened.

Some contemporary writers like to argue that before Wolfenden, before the reform of the law, there was almost a paradise of casual sex where you didn't have to identify yourself, a sort of contemporary queer argument that you could just be, and do, without having to have an identity – and some people see modern identity as a complete trap. But for me and my generation, escaping from that amorphousness, that casualness and the illegality of it, was a liberation, because it allowed us to express our identity.

GRIFF:
I remember at six o'clock in the morning in the central lobby [of the House of Commons] when somebody came up to Antony Grey, who at the time ran the Albany Trust, and said, "Well, aren't you happy?" and he said, "No, we're only halfway there." He said it would take another ten years, but it actually took much longer to get where we are.

EMMANUEL:
Then there was the changing of the act in '67 and I realised how significant that was, in the way that it decriminalised all the things I did. I thought the 1967 law reform was fantastic. I knew it was going to mean something, I didn't know what but I knew it was going to mean something, because you could do what we were doing openly and honestly. It was sort of a coming out and at the time that all tied in with the advent of Gay Liberation.

4

COMING OUT AND GOING OUT:
LONDON NIGHTLIFE

The stories in this chapter are about bars and clubs in London. There were, of course, other lesbian and gay watering holes in other cities in Britain during the period covered in this book, but the vast majority were to be found in the capital.

During the interviews that I conducted, I quickly realised that asking a gay man or a lesbian, "What bars did you go to when you were younger?", has a different implication than asking straight people the same thing. This question signifies so much more than "Where did you enjoy socialising and having a drink at the weekend?" For us, the very discovery of those bars and clubs was often nothing less than a life-saving event. We weren't just after a pint and a bit of a bop. By even setting foot in a gay bar or club we were doing something extremely important, we were seeking out other people like us. We were looking for 'similar'. We generally didn't see 'similar' in our workplaces, our neighbourhoods, or our family environments, so we would go to extraordinary lengths to find the names and addresses of lesbian and gay bars that sometimes would end up being hidden away in a basement or down an unlikely looking alleyway. And when we got in the bar, we weren't even necessarily there for the purpose of finding a potential partner. One of the main reasons for seeking out such a place was that we wanted to know we were not alone.

Sometimes, however, the utopia we had spent so long

imagining proved a bit of a disappointment. As we caressed our drink, we would look around hopefully and wait for something to happen. We probably weren't sure what it would be, but we would certainly know it if it came along. But instead of a world-shattering experience, we might have remained on our own, speaking to no-one else all evening. There might have been a polite but professionally distant person serving at the bar and possibly a couple of women in a corner booth, either in the middle of a heated break-up, or not talking, or maybe just looking as uncomfortable as we felt. OK, I know I'm not painting a wonderful picture here, and these examples have been taken from my own experiences rather than those of the contributors (whom I hope had slightly better luck) but what we had wanted in that elusive lesbian or gay bar was nothing less than a fanfare announcing that we had come to the right place and that from that moment on we would be cared for in the bosom of the lesbian and gay community.

But whatever our experiences, good or bad, if you ask almost any older lesbian or gay man to tell you about the bars and clubs they frequented when they were younger, their eyes will glaze over with fond remembrance of those particular times and places. I have used this subject to break the ice with groups of older LGB people as a reminiscence topic in theatre work and it never fails to instigate immediate and animated conversations between the participants, who talk with delight and humour about the various places they have frequented over the years.

Bars and clubs have been of immense historic importance to lesbians and gay men. The Stonewall movement itself was of course named after the gay bar in Greenwich Village in New York where, on a Friday evening in June 1969, the police raided The Stonewall Inn. Contrary to expectations, the patrons fought back, provoking three nights of rioting in the area accompanied by the appearance of 'Gay Power' slogans on the buildings and, almost overnight, the grassroots of the Gay Liberation Movement were born.

The London clubs, pubs and bars mentioned in this chapter stretch over a period that dates from the early 1940s to the mid 1990s. Over that time not only their character, but also their level of visibility and accessibility changed dramatically – to a point where some gay pubs in the latter half of that period were advertising their presence with rainbow flags outside. The men's establishments ranged from private members' clubs like The Colony Club and The Rockingham, mentioned by Stanley, where gay men were welcomed from the 1940s onwards, to pubs in the East End and elsewhere where drag was the regular form of entertainment, referred to by Ron and Roger. There were (and still are) several gay men's pubs in London around the areas of Soho and Earls Court. Cyril and other contributors refer to The Coleherne in Old Brompton Road which opened in 1866 and became a gay pub in the mid-1950s.[1] Originally it was segregated into two bars, one for the straight crowd and one for the gay community, at a time when homosexuality was illegal. In the 1970s it became a notorious leather bar, with men wearing chaps and leather jackets with key chains and colour-coded handkerchiefs.

As for the women contributors, when asked about bars and clubs, stories about The Gateways club were the most prolific. 'The Gates' (as it was referred to) was situated off the Kings Road in Chelsea and was one of the few places in the country where lesbians could meet openly during the 1940s and up until the mid Eighties. It opened in 1930, becoming a members' club in 1936, and by 1967 it was women-only. Lesbians and bisexuals sought out The Gateways, as did curious heterosexuals, and for many women a visit was their first introduction to lesbian life. In 1963 the Minorities Research Group (mentioned further in Chapter Seven) was founded and members were recruited from amongst The Gateways clientele. This again shows that pubs and clubs for gay people were more than just drinking venues. They were a way to find out about other groups and relevant political movements. By the 1980s, however, there were far more gay and lesbian venues opening up in central London and the fashion was for large discos, so after a period of opening only three nights a week for a while, The Gateways finally closed its doors in 1985.

But even though the existence of The Gateways club was clearly important in the history of London lesbians (myself included), not all its clients were enamoured of that particular venue. Vito recalls that she thought *"Gateways was rough"* and *"pretty scary"* and that she *"just went down for curiosity's sake"*. Carol mentions another club called The Casino, where she says, *"You got gays in there, runaways who'd run away from home for being gay and been thrown out,"* which demonstrates that clubs and pubs were also regarded as places of refuge for those who felt cast out by the rest of society. Many more pubs and clubs are named in the following chapter by contributors who frequented them over several decades, and they were all clearly seen as being an integral part of gay men's and lesbians' lifestyles. About one of the particular pubs, Ron says, *"People came there and we felt we had a right to be considered. We're not different. You could recharge your batteries."* To refer to these places as lifelines is probably not an exaggeration.

CS

~

Interviews

Early Lesbian and Gay Pubs and Clubs

STANLEY:
I drank heavily in those days and I was always in these clubs and bars and God knows what, and of course I was very keen on low company and I knew one or two contacts, because in those days it was rather smart to have friends in the low world. In Piccadilly Circus, in the old days there was a huge place called The Billiard Room. It's where the Virgin store is now. There were the Soho Billiard Halls, full of terrible people! I used to go there with a great friend of mine, he was most unstable, and he was very fond of me. I used to pick up all sorts of people. He would play billiards and I would watch and of course there were all these ruffians and gentlemen as well. But I wasn't interested in picking up somebody gay, I was interested in picking up somebody who would comply. It was all done with charm and chat. I had amazing success and then I would take them back to my flat, because I had this big flat on the corner of Berkeley

Square, huge flat. I had ten rooms, two bathrooms and the rent was about £600 a year.

DAN:
Clubs in London were wonderful in those days, in the late Forties. There were marvellous clubs run by women who had a great affection for gays and the famous one was Muriel Belcher who ran the famous club in Soho, The Colony Club. But the best club of all was The Rockingham. That was elegant. You could take your mother down there. Archer Street. They were very fussy. You couldn't take anyone in in uniform. There was a doorman and a man at the desk and you wouldn't get in there unless you'd paid your subscription. You couldn't bring people in off the street. They were very selective. Fresh flowers, beautiful antiques.

STANLEY:
The Rockingham was started by a friend of mine who I knew at Oxford and it had a membership of some twenty or thirty thousand from all over the world. He was taken to court for running a gay club. The judge said, "Sir, you seem to have nothing but male members in your club." But my friend just said, "I think you would find the same thing in White's or Boodle's." Because the St James's clubs are full of men. So he got away with it. How could they argue? All the men's clubs are for men.

LEONARD:
I used to go to the bars, there were about six or seven gay clubs. There was The Rockingham and another one called The A&B, a gay wartime thing, that was in the middle of Soho. There was a famous one in Piccadilly, The White Bear. There wasn't really a gay scene but when the police came in everyone changed the conversation. There was a famous bar called The Fitzroy, off

Tottenham Court Road, jammed full. People like Danny Kaye would come there. It was an amazing place.

You know The Golden Lion in Soho? I met someone there once who was very aggressive and dominant and bossy and butch. He'd just been to the races and he had a huge pile of notes and he said to me, "Where are you going?" I said I was going home and he said, "No you're not, you're staying with me." We went to a restaurant and then to a gambling bar on Shaftesbury Avenue, where they seemed to know him, and then we got home at three or four in the morning. He wanted to stay in a hotel but I said he could stay with me so we came back here by taxi and in the morning he said, "I'll see you again at 2.30." He was glamorous, and very aggressive.

So at 2.30 the phone went and he said, "Where the hell are you? I'm in a hotel, The Hilton. Get here." So I jumped into a taxi and he was there, stripped to the waist, and he said, "You sit over there and I'll be with you in a minute." So he went to the bathroom and suddenly he came out dressed in drag and he said, "I know you like uniforms so I got this for you." I used to be very friendly with a lot of soldiers. But he was dressed as a matron. I was so bored, I hate drag, hate it. Loathe it. And what was extraordinary about the room was he had a mirror behind the door and I had a feeling he'd been there before and he put on some stockings and said, "You are a lucky devil, you're a lucky bastard..." going on and on.

IAN:
First club that I ever knew was a gay club which was, funnily enough, run by two Edinburgh ladies, May and Josie Adair, who were terribly polite and said things like, "Josie, will you take the bucket down the stairs, there's been a stabbing on the doorstep." It was in the middle of Soho, this club, and it was called The Toucan. If you looked at the books you'd see a very respectable, mixed turnover, because there were journalists and actors and actresses and so on. There were, I should think, one third journalists, one third gay men and one third lesbians,

and they had the odd famous person to add respectability to it. Sybil Thorndyke used to come in there sometimes.

It was also in the days when drinking was sort of a strategic business, because pub hours were very limited but when you were turned out of the pub at three o'clock you could go along to The Toucan, because their drinking hours started at three o'clock. So people could drink right round the clock if they knew where to go and what to do and The Toucan was very useful to some people for this purpose. It was useful to others because it had gay people there as well. So that was my first experience of a gay pub as such.

CYRIL:
My friend Gordon said, "I'll take you to The Coleherne," which is the most famous, oldest gay bar in London. It was completely leather and it was notorious as being the leather bar. So I was there in my sports jacket and flannels and the place was just full of denim and leather. I suppose I was alarmed really, but I remember being very excited looking around at all the guys, being very butch and all that kind of thing – and I'm fairly butch but I was intimidated, I think, by all the leather and feeling no part of it. Here am I, gay, but I'm not in the scene. I was an outsider as I've been all my life. It was very strange.

CAROL:
Living in Dagenham was pretty awful because it was factory fodder. I didn't fit into any of it. So in 1962 I saw this advertisement for a trainee manageress to come and work in London and you got a bedsitter with the job. First of all I worked in Mayfair and then I transferred over to Notting Hill Gate. My flat was in Brompton Road. I was seventeen then. There was this woman called Mrs French, lovely lady, she was like a mother to me and she said, "There's a pub over there called The Fiesta." It was a big thing in the Fifties, early Sixties, Notting Hill Gate. "Carol," she said, "don't have anything to

do with those people." And I said, "What do you mean, Mrs French?" She said, "They're queers." So I said, "What does that mean?" And she said it was a club where gay men and women went in drag, and not in drag, and there were criminals and convicts, blacks and everything and she said, "Oh, you want to keep away from all them." So of course I wanted to go down there!

JENNY:
There was a gay club in Notting Hill Gate called The Fiesta Club, down in some basement. This was about 1962. It was full of smoke and stank of beer and it was mostly populated by prostitutes and dirty old men and drug dealers. Some gay boys, but mainly a den of iniquity. I had a wild flatmate at the time who sort of went on the game and took drugs and generally behaved quite badly. She knew about this place and dragged us all down there for somewhere to go. She wasn't gay – just a loose woman really. One night I winked at some old dyke, not knowing that a wink meant, "I want to sleep with you." Anyway this woman talked in a cockney accent and said she "worked on a barrow in Portobello Market, darlin'". So I ended up working with her myself on Saturdays to supplement my photographic day job, shouting out things like, "Lovely nanas. Two bob a pahnd," which was great, and I got ten shillings, which was quite a lot of money in those days, and all the fruit I could carry.

In those days you were either butch or femme. Because I didn't dress particularly butch they would ask, "Are you butch or femme?" And I sort of um'd and ah'd and said, "Well, perhaps I'm a bit of both."

"Well, you can't be both darlin', you've got to be one or the other."

And I said, "Well, in that case, I'm butch."

"You don't look butch!"

"Well, I'll try 'arder," I said, trying to talk dahn-market but not succeeding frightfully well.

So I used to wear a pleated skirt to minimise my big hips, and a tie. Of course the effect was completely ghastly and nobody believed I was butch and it didn't really work anyway.

The Gateways

CAROL:
One night some friends took me to The Gateways and of course that was an eye-opener for me. Oh God, it was awful, it was terrible! I was really nervous, first gay club, meeting other gay women. I remember going down that stairs and Gina being on the door and on the left were all the butch women in drag and on the right were all the women in dresses. It was really scary. You just didn't know what to do with yourself. You felt really awkward and all these butch women were asking me to dance and you couldn't say no, you know? You were just glad to be there. And so it was good but it was scary, it was frightening, it was just mind-blowing really.

But they weren't that friendly at The Gateways. I didn't like Gina at all, she was aggressive, she just wanted your money. Smithy was nice. She was the one that lived with Gina. It was very cliquey. There were all the gay women and they all hung around Smithy playing cards at the bar. You were young coming in, you didn't fit into it all and the music was naff, you had a jukebox and you had to put money in to play the bloody music!

STANLEY:
There was a famous girls' club which I was taken to with some difficulty called The Gateways... rather dangerous because dykes in a rage can be rather nasty.

VITO:
I thought Gateways was rough. I just went down for curiosity's sake. There was something about the layout, you'd be at the

top of these really high steps and you can look down into it and Smithy was on the door, quite a bulky tough woman, and that was pretty scary. There was another place called The Robin which was small, nicely lit, it had nice coloured lights around the bar and it had a really nice jukebox and a table-tennis table in the back and these nice round seats and nice comfortable chairs with candles burning and everything. Whereas The Gateways was sort of ranch-style wooden benches and a bit of a dancefloor in the middle and much more heavy drinking sort of culture. If you went to the loo it was freezing cold and I can remember a woman standing there combing her hair with Brylcreem. Plus, it didn't seem to be a social place where you could make friends if you didn't go down with somebody, whereas at The Robin, people would talk to you.

And of course there was the Gateway grind. That was the only dance most people knew. One leg goes between the legs so that your hips are adjoining and it's a sort of a swaying movement, usually to a slow dance, so you're really in a clinch and one puts their arms round the neck of another, or can hold you in the dance stance. Or you'd be leaning on the other person's shoulder but leaning very close and just rubbing yourself against each other basically!

Pubs and Clubs in the Sixties

CAROL:
Through living at Earls Court, getting on the scene, I found out about The Boltons and The Coleherne. They were gay pubs. The Boltons was on the corner of Earls Court Road, then you cross over and then there was The Coleherne. The gay men'll tell you, they all wore leather gear in there or jean gear. But The Boltons was more open and gay women would go in there more, it was a mixed sort of a pub where they used to do drag once a week with the Trollettes and people like that. They were a duo, one did Streisand and one did Liza Minnelli. They were fabulous, they really were. So they'd come on a Friday night

and we'd go in there and drink. It was a social place where everyone would drink, in there.

The Casino was a West End club off Wardour Streeet. It was a basement sort of a place. It was one of those places that was everything. You got gays in there, runaways who'd run away from home for being gay and been thrown out. You got prostitutes, you got touts, you got crooks, drug dealers, pimps. There was kidnapping going on and all sorts but you felt comfortable because everyone accepted everybody, and you accepted them for whatever they were. They played all reggae, Blue Beat it was called in those days, it was like a Jamaican reggae. There was no alcohol. It was like American style, coffee, teas, Coca-Cola and drugs. Lots of heroin going around and dope. You name it, it was there. But it was a great place to be, you felt comfortable, and lots of girls started to come there from all over the country – and that went on for about, I don't know, five or six years, in the early Sixties. And the guy who ran it was an ex-copper and he was now a drug dealer, so that was fun as well!

There was probably about twenty of us that used to come and go, and it was open all night, so you could stay there all night if you wanted to. You paid an entrance fee, about two bob, one and six, very cheap, you'd pay that to go in. There was a little bar with teas and coffee and seats down each side. The prostitutes, if they fancied it, they'd go off with a girl. At that time it was very fashionable to be gay. Although it didn't seem so in the media, it was, and if you were in drag you could have your pick of women.

And another night there, Ronnie, who knew me, he said, "Caz," he said, "Guess what?" He said, "Dusty Springfield's upstairs." I said, "Oh, is she going to come down?" He said, "No, she's having a party." 'Cos she lived just up by Baker Street then. My girlfriend lived opposite her. Now, Dusty wouldn't really go to the clubs. She went to The Gates when it was shut. They used to open it especially for her. I wasn't there but a girl I knew who worked there told me that when Dusty used to come down they'd shut it and when the club was shut Dusty would go in about twelve or one o'clock with a crowd and they'd open it up for her. So no-one really saw her, only the people who worked there and Gina and Smithy and all that. So Ron said, "She's sent people down and she's picked you out and she wants you to come to her party." I said, "Oh fuck off!" He said, "Caz, I'm telling you, it's true. She's upstairs. She's got a great big Rolls Royce." So I went to look and there was a Rolls Royce up there and she was rounding up girls to go to a party at her place in Baker Street.

Anyway I didn't go. I think I was frightened really. It was a bit strange. I mean you've got this idol, and I loved Dusty, but I wouldn't know what to do or say. I'd go all silly, you know? So I chickened out, and I was sorry, because some of the other girls went and I heard they all had a great time, and I wish I'd have gone anyway.

PETER B:
In the early to mid Sixties it was all a bit diverse because there was The Coleherne, which was fairly awful then, and The Boltons was gay. Earls Court was always rather seedy. There was The Calabash in Fulham, Chelsea, with a coffee bar and a restaurant called The Casserole. Then there was The Festival, The A&B, The Apollo and the As You Like It. The Festival was in Brydges Place, which runs down the side of the Coliseum, and that was a key club. You let yourself in with your key. The Festival was definitely gay. A pub we used to use which was very mixed was The Salisbury in St Martin's Lane, mixed gay and theatrical. The As You Like It was high bohemian and that was a coffee bar that was open very late and that's where I first encountered people like Quentin Crisp and Lindsay Kemp and Long John Baldry.

A bit later there was a club called Le Duce, which I became manager of, and that was kind of ambiguous straight men who were trying to decide and usually tipped over. Straight women who didn't particularly like straight men. Young dykes and young gay men and it was sort of Carnaby Street. Sex was one of the driving impetuses, but at Le Duce, you'd go there on a Saturday night in your Carnaby outfit, hipster trousers and those funny little French sweaters that showed your midriff, and you would perhaps meet someone and you'd dance and it's quite likely you'd arrange to meet in the week and go to the pictures together. With a lot of the West End pubs and coffee bars it was very working-class youths, so the places weren't licensed. It was coffee and orange juice and drinking milk and speed, and the drinking clubs like the Apollo and Carousel and A&B were primarily populated by older people and rentboys.

The kind of scene I moved in was young and that was Carnaby Street, which was very, very affordable. John Stephen, when he got going, knew how to make clothes cheaply and sell them cheaply, so cheap that you could go back every week and get a new outfit for the weekend. And that percolated around a lot of those clubs, and when clubs started to get late licences, those people who'd been at Le Duce in 1965, by 1970 would probably be at Yours Or Mine in Kensington High Street. That was a supper club, downstairs, and you were given a ticket when you went in and the theory was that you'd have supper, which would be a hard-boiled egg or something. But that gave them the excuse to be able to serve liquor. There was a similar club in Earls Court called The Masquerade which had a proper restaurant attached.

At Le Duce people like David Hockney were regulars, people like Ossie Clark, David Bowie, Jagger, used to go to Yours Or Mine, and then Bang! opened much later down the line, in the Eighties, as the first really enormous venue in London that attracted straight people and celebrities as well.

RON & ROGER:

Roger: In the early Sixties when we came back to London there had been quite a revolution here because you'd had the Beatles and *That Was The Week That Was* and so things were opening up a bit, but people were still fairly circumspect about clubs.

Ron: There was The Festival Club which was round the back of the ENO. Then there was the A&B one, which was a drinking club in what is now Chinatown. Once you were in, everybody knew, but you were kind of careful about being seen going in. The A&B was essentially a place to drink but it was a pick-up place of course.

Roger: Down an alley in what's now Chinatown, up a staircase, and I think it was only on one floor. I think it was about four rooms, if that.

Ron: And you had to sign in and of course everyone did a squiggle.

Roger: There was no dancing.

Ron: We were still illegal.

Roger: This was 1963 and '4.

Ron: You could drink, you talk, you socialise, but no dancing...

Roger: No touching.

Ron: Because the police could raid at any time.

Roger: In 1963 there were public houses that did drag shows.

Ron: And that was a coded thing for guys to go to.

Roger: It would be mostly gays and the chap I was working for had a motor car and he took us occasionally on a Saturday evening...

Ron: To Daniel Farson's place on the Isle of Dogs. The Waterman's Arms.

Roger: And The Aberdeen at Bethnal Green.

Ron: In a way Daniel Farson's place on the Isle of Dogs was sufficiently far away from the centre of London. It was crowded. You had to fight your way in. There was an old actress there named Ida Barr who would sing, "Just like the old ivy on the garden wall clinging so tightly..." That was her big number. She was a real old musical star. Rogers and Star was one act. Lee and

Dodo was a couple and their gags were like: "On the underground there was sailor. She nearly fainted and I had a stroke." And all this rubbish. So the crowd was mixed, predominantly gay. And the biggest mistake you could make was to take on these artists because you'd get: "Put your handbag down and come up here, dear," and all this. And it was kind of liberating because you felt, "Yes!" You could fight back. People came there and we felt we had a right to be considered. We're not different. You could recharge your batteries.

EMMANUEL:

There was the Arts and Battledress club, which was an old club, dating back from after the war. It was in Soho just near The Blue Post, up some stairs and on the top floor, and it was for people who went in suits and collars and ties and it was very packed at the weekend. They had a big thick book called The Book, in which people wrote their comments about where to go, which was an international gay travelogue as well as a travelogue to Britain and it showed where places were sympathetic. You asked the barman, "Could I look at the book?"

RON & ROGER

Ron: Then there was The Spartan which was piss elegant.

Roger: It had writing tables and stuff. It was a gentleman's club.

Ron: And then there was The Festival which again was a kind of theatrical drinking place.

Roger: That was a very relaxed atmosphere. The chap behind the bar was a resting actor and you could talk to other people. But there was no dancing, no touching. It really was just a place to drink.

Ron: But you could relax to some extent and know the person to whom you were speaking was of like mind. How did we find out?

Roger: Someone would tell you.

Ron: Because there were so few places to go, they were common currency.

Pubs and Clubs in the Seventies

CAROL:

In the Seventies, things got a lot better generally, clubs started springing up. There was Louisa's supper club in Wardour Street. It was a man in drag, a queen, French, and she started this club and you paid a couple of quid to go in, it was quite expensive. It was open till three, Friday and Saturday nights, and it was mixed. But to get a licence they had to provide a Spam salad or something – supper club, you see? Louisa's was very, very popular. You had to queue to get in 'cos it was the only place at that time. It was great because au pairs were coming to London then, so you'd get a lot of au pairs and foreign girls and queens, so it was a great atmosphere. You had a lot of Spanish at that time because of Franco; it was terrible to be gay in Spain. They shot you, virtually.

So Louisa's was an eye opener and after that there was The White Raven in Bayswater, which two gay women I knew started up. It was a basement place that was nice, only at the weekend, as well. Then there was The Mother Redcap in Herne Hill: that was nice, a great big night and they had a Friday night and it was packed with women from everywhere and that was brilliant. Then there was The Black Cap in Camden. Then there was The Aztec in Bayswater, that was fun. The music was really good, that was soul, 'cos we liked soul, Motown, and it was all painted white. You'd get some very trendy women down there and women were dressing down, more casual and growing their hair. There was Yours Or Mine or The Sombrero, it was called, either one, that was in Kensington High Street. That was a mixed place, straights and gays.

BOB C:

I remember going to this gay bar once back in Edinburgh and thinking, "Thank God I moved to London!" It was just so depressed. I lived in Notting Hill Gate so there were bars around and maybe in the late Sixties they would have been more discreet, but by the time I was going, 1972/3, they were more open. There was a place called The Catacombs in Earls Court and this was in a cellar and it had a music night and stayed open till after eleven and they didn't sell any alcohol but you could go there and cruise and dance and so on. And I suppose it's in The Catacombs that I began to understand the whole issue of cruising, of men looking for one another, making eye contact or not making eye contact.

In the mid Seventies you began to get better places to go to. There was a guy called Tricky Dicky who used to run discos on Friday evening and Saturday evening in rooms above bars and they were really quite nice and so, from the success of that, people began to rent bigger rooms in bigger discos. Then in the mid Seventies the first big disco in London, Bang!, opened. It was on a Monday night at The Astoria and that was like nothing we'd ever known before 'cos it wasn't particularly political and it wasn't just a small sort of place, it was enormous. And then of course there was Heaven later on. But in the late Seventies, early Eighties, there was just this blossoming of places and sometimes you did get ripped off, sometimes the service wasn't all that great, but you just had so much more choice then. In some ways it made it much more possible for you to compartmentalise your desire. When you were involved with GLF [Gay Liberation Front] you were trying to come to terms with your sexuality and the politics of it but then in the Seventies these big discos and clubs meant that you could forget about the politics really and you could just enjoy it.

5

THE SHAME OF IT ALL

I am aware that a chapter even partly devoted to the subject of shame in regard to homosexuality might initially seem a little disturbing, but in the interviews I have conducted, several older gay men and lesbians have referred to their personal experiences about their own sexuality with a certain degree of shame and I feel that this area merits closer examination.

As mentioned in the Introduction, in 2011 I worked on a theatrical project called *Staying Out Late* which involved older LGBT people discussing their fears and concerns with regard to the professional care they might receive later in life in their own home, sheltered housing or a residential home. Conversations that arose in the workshops covered topics such as whether the participants would ideally like to live in a solely gay or lesbian care home and if they would prefer to have gay or lesbian carers. Some people just expressed the hope that the existing care system would do enough work to ensure they were not marginalised, did not experience prejudice and were not forced to become invisible because of their sexual orientation. They hoped their history would be understood as being different from that of their heterosexual peers.

I mention this project because, in listening to participants' opinions and attitudes, I perceived an element of shame around their sexuality. This shame may have been from old feelings and experiences or from internalised homophobia. This is an issue that straight care home managers and carers will have to engage with themselves before they can even begin to comprehend how the older gay and lesbian people in their care might react to being asked any questions about their sexual orientation.

As discussed earlier in this book, the realisation very early on that we, as gay people, are somehow different from others is often cloaked in a degree of secrecy. This is because instinctively we feel that it is potentially dangerous for us to be different from the rest of the pack, the class, the family, the neighbours, and sadly that realisation of our differentness is then sometimes clouded with shame.

We are not born with feelings of shame around our sexuality or sexual orientation. For some of us, the shame emerges when we reveal to someone else what we feel or think, and have them react in an adverse way, whether that person is a close friend or a parent, a member of our church or the object of our desires. Others might have heard of negative reactions to someone else's coming out or seen a newspaper headline making someone's sexual orientation a scandalous matter, or they might even just have an inner sense of shame for feeling different and outside the norm. Rarely did (or do) any of us come out to be met with approval, celebration and party-planning suggestions.

Modern attitudes toward homosexuality have religious, legal and medical underpinnings and all of these factors contribute to how gay men and lesbians regard themselves. Before the Middle Ages, homosexual acts appear to have been tolerated or ignored by the Christian church throughout Europe, but from the twelfth century onwards, hostility towards homosexuality spread when religious and secular institutions and religious teachings became incorporated into legal sanctions. By the end of the nineteenth century, medicine and psychiatry were effectively competing with religion and the law for jurisdiction over sexuality. This historical shift was generally considered progressive because a sick person was less blameworthy than a sinner or criminal.[1]

Although sexual behaviour in private between adult men was decriminalised in England and Wales in 1967, treatments to change homosexuals into heterosexuals peaked in the 1960s and early 1970s. By this time a procedure known as aversion therapy had become one of the more popular methods used to 'cure' sexual deviation, including homosexuality and cross-dressing. Aversion therapy is a form of behaviour modification that employs unpleasant and sometimes painful stimuli in an effort to help a patient unlearn socially unacceptable or harmful behaviour. The intention of this practice was to replace sexual arousal with noxious stimuli so that the patient would rid himself of his sexual deviation and develop 'normal' desires. Bob L describes how, when he was in his twenties and feared that he might be a homosexual, he went to his doctor about his concerns and elected to have aversion therapy. He tells of how he *"underwent this so-called therapy, which was the most barbaric thing I've ever known"*.

The American Psychiatric Association officially declassified homosexuality as a mental illness in 1974 but it wasn't until 1992 that the World Health Organisation followed suit.

Another subject touched upon in this chapter is the reaction of our families to the news that we are lesbians or gay men. But one thing I have personally found about families is that they can often surprise us. Some family members, as shown in the stories in this chapter, whether parents or children, have been surprisingly accepting and others have been quite condemnatory when we have least suspected they would be. Sue had thought that her Quaker parents would be fine about her telling them she was a lesbian but instead they reacted in an extremely prejudiced manner. She recalls, *"My dad said, 'We request that thee doesn't tell thy brothers or our relatives.'"* But we also hear uplifting stories about family members who have responded in a positive and encouraging way. A part of me delights in hearing such tales and finds them extremely moving, but another part of me is still cross that we sometimes hold ourselves hostage to parents or other loved ones and allow them the power to make or break us by their reaction to what we cannot help but be.

Finally, there are a few comments about people facing and dealing with their particular religion's attitude to homosexuality. Reconciling one's religion with one's sexual orientation continues to be one of the most difficult things many gay men and lesbians struggle with. Rex recalls that during the 1950s, at the time of the 'witch-hunts' against homosexuals, he and his boyfriend sought out advice from a vicar who rather unhelpfully told them both that *"there was nothing wrong with being gay and in love with another man, but you don't touch"*.

I think it would be fair to say that, compared to many other nations, Britain is not one of the most actively religious countries in the world. If these interviews had been collected in a predominantly Catholic, Hindu, or Muslim country, there would, I am sure, have been far more comments offered around this subject matter. Many gay men and lesbians have, over the years, been maligned by or invisible to most mainstream religions, but there are now several religious denominations around the country that affirm us and welcome us as full members of their communities.

But given that, in previous decades, religion, society, family and even the medical world were telling lesbians and gay men that their behaviour and feelings were abnormal and wrong, it would be surprising, if not miraculous, if today's older LGB people did not have some feelings of shame around their sexual orientation. Jeffrey reminds us that homosexuality *"was not only sinful and sick, it was also illegal, and probably all of those three"*.

CS

~

Interviews

Shame

EMMANUEL:
There was one terrible incident which really, to this day, I feel utterly, utterly ashamed of in so many ways... There was a friend of the family, a woman, and she was about three or four years older than me, and this was when I was about fourteen. We were standing outside and I must have been standing with my arms or wrists slightly limp and she said, "What are you standing like that for, with your arms held like that? You look

like a sissy." And I was so mortified that she should say that and somehow identify what I was. I felt that this was such a feeling of exposure and ridicule for who I was. I could never ever conceive of telling my family that I could be "like that", whatever "like that" was. Very, very conflicting and difficult and I think that one became very lonely through that.

SARAH:

When I was seven I was packed off to a boarding school on the south coast, and I was there for eleven years and during that time I became absolutely certain that I was gay. I used to sing for the school when I got older and I think I showed an interest (this is an understatement) in another girl when I was about fourteen, and I was put into a private room, a little room of my own. Nothing was said. I'd been in a dormitory and they put me into this room where nobody ever slept on their own except a girl who wet the bed. She was on one side and on the other side was the red stocking room, where they used to hang the stockings after we played lacrosse, and it stank and it was horrible. It made me feel dirty, nasty, and there was nobody to talk to. Nobody.

I made the best of it but it was horrible and none of the people that I used to sleep with in the dormitory, the other girls, they didn't say anything either. They didn't make life difficult at all for me, they just kept me in this room which was horrible, until I was eighteen. So it's terrible when there's a silence about something and then to have to go on with your life and pretend that nothing had happened. It was dreadful because nothing was said but I knew why I'd been put in that room and I think that that is why I'm not able to say the 'L' word.

I'm not at all proud to be gay but I'm very proud of my husband and my children for accepting me for what I am. I think that possibly I should never have got married. I'm sure that I hurt my husband on the way. And this thing about school, being in this little room.

JEFFREY:

I first came to London as a student and first started having sex, gay sex, in London in the mid Sixties – and of course it was before the law changed so I was still illegal, whatever I did. It didn't stop me or my generation having sex but it was always in a sense constrained by this awareness that you could fall into disaster. Because, of course, all the stories that you read were of disasters, lives ending after being caught cottaging, all the famous queer novels in the Fifties ending in suicide and so on. So there was always that sense of disaster just waiting for you. We all knew it was illegal. That was just part of the air you breathed. It was not only sinful and sick, it was also illegal, and probably all of those three. If you weren't religious and you weren't having psychological problems about it, the fact that it was illegal was a real inhibition.

CAROL:

When I was four I had my first girlfriend and I remember getting into trouble. We used to play in the grass and her mum stopped her seeing me and I didn't know what that was about. But she'd seen us playing on the grass together and there was something that she thought was awful and I was a bad influence. I was very upset by it because we'd spent a lot of time together, because she lived about three doors away and we had a really big garden and we used to play all sorts of games there, Cowboys and Indians with our friends, but her mother just stopped her coming out. It was terrible. But I suppose perhaps she saw something that I didn't see. I don't know.

NORMA:

A lot of black people scorn the idea of being gay. I mean this thing of calling it 'a white man's disease', especially with men. I've heard people say, "That's something that they do here, they never did that in my country," and we all know that's a load of rubbish!

JENNY:

When I was at school I thought, there must be other people like me, but it'll take me a very long amount of time to find them and I've got to be very careful – because I knew it was very wrong.

I don't know if people were frightened or were holding a mirror held up to themselves but whenever anything gay was ever mentioned everybody went, "Ugh, ugh, ugh!" And I know I did it myself to cover my tracks because I was so afraid that anyone 'normal' would think that I was a lesbian and I knew that they'd run out of the room or I'd lose jobs. People wouldn't want to work with me or they'd snigger and laugh. It was very much a double life and I can't think how one managed it.

None of my family knew, except for my little sister. I told her when I was about twenty-two. She was very upset, because she'd obviously read snippets in the *Sun* or something like that about these people 'living in a twilight world' and so knew that I was in for a life of 'total misery'. That's what it was seen to be because we had no positive images at all, ever. We had no role models, did we? Were there any role models? I can only think of Rosa Klebb, this lesbian in an early Bond movie, who had retractable spikes in her boots. Charming. But I can't think of any others. Occasionally there would be a "Disgusting Lesbian Lust!" type headline in the *Sun* or something, and all would go, "Ugh, ugh, ugh!" So you knew you'd be in trouble if you didn't keep quiet. I suppose Martina was the first person who publicly came out and of course my mother hated her with a deep passion because she was: "A LESBIAN! And proud of it." But I was used to that kind of remark because you sort of knew that your role in life was to be the Worst Person in the World.

BOB L:

When I was twenty-four I had aversion therapy. I came out of the RAF and all my contemporaries were marrying, settling down, and I thought, "Well, wouldn't it be so much easier if I did?" So I went to my GP who didn't allow me to rush into it, he didn't know much about it but he knew, well he had some idea, that it was going to be pretty horrible. Anyway, eventually he made an appointment with a psychiatrist in Harley Street and all I remember about that was this beautifully furnished office with rosewood cabinets. I don't know why I remember these things! And this man who was immaculately dressed with glittering gold glasses. But I don't remember him asking me any questions about why. All he wanted was his twenty-five guineas fee, which, when I was on five pounds a week, was quite a lot of money, but I found it somehow. And so that entailed going into an annexe at Charing Cross Hospital – and then the annexe was on Hampstead Heath (which I didn't associate with anything then of course) – where I underwent this so-called therapy, which was the most barbaric thing I've ever known.

What they did was, you go in and you have daily sessions. I think one a day, about a couple of hours, and during that session you're taken into a tiny cell-like room with electric fires all around. Before you go in you're given an injection of Pentothal, which is supposedly the truth drug, and some other drug. And then when you go in, as I say, there are all these electric fires round in this tiny room and a nurse comes in and you have to keep drinking a warm saline solution and in the meantime she shows you pictures of men doing things and the idea is that you associate that with being sick. And I just learned to play the game. I thought, you know, "I'll get this session over."

I kept making myself... well, I didn't need to make myself sick because these pills in the water did. Anyway, it meant that while I was in there, it was five days I think... and I couldn't sleep and when I did I was having terrible nightmares.

So anyway, that was in the mid Sixties when barbiturates and pills were the answer to everything. Apparently nobody knew the side effects or anything so I was just put onto barbiturates and they were very strong ones. So what with that and the alcohol, I was on those for many years and that's when I had this episode at home, when I tried to finish it. I was still living at home and I'd had enough of everything, so as soon as I got home, I had a bottle of whisky in my room and some barbiturates and I just took the lot. That was Sunday lunchtime and I woke up with my mother sitting at my hospital bed on Friday evening. I was out completely.

Family Reactions

CAROL:

I grew up in Dagenham, where Ford's is. It was the biggest council estate in Europe. It was very depressing there, a very straight scene. I joined the library, you were allowed to join it when you were eleven, and I was trying to find myself so I read all Freud's books and psychology stuff.

My mum used to say, "Carol, why are you reading all that stuff?"

So I said, "Well Mum, I'm trying to find myself."

She said, "What do you mean?"

I said, "Well, I think I'm different to everybody else."

"No you're not. There's nothing different about you. If you keep on reading those books then you will imagine you're one of those people."

And I said to her, "But Mum, I think I'm a lesbian."

"Oh no, you're not. No, you're not." Just shoved it under the carpet completely.

After I moved to London I didn't go home for quite a while but when I did go home, because I missed my family, especially my mum, I went home in full drag. My dad had been in the navy, he didn't say a word. I think my dad was a bit queeny anyway. I took a few girls home with me too and as I was going out the door my mum said, "I don't want you coming home any more."

So I said, "Why, Mum? What have I done?"

She said, "You're a very bad influence on your younger brother and sister."

My sister was eighteen months old, my brother was five, and my mum said that I was a bad influence on them! So

I said, "OK," and that was it then. So I didn't go home for about four years, that's when I went to live in Manchester. And then I decided, "This is ridiculous, this drag thing," and that's when I started to dress down, for my own sake really, for me. I wanted to be accepted in the community, if you like. Because it was a lot of pressure and it was so difficult in them days to find places to live. Everywhere you went there were signs up saying: "No Blacks, No Homosexuals, No Irish, No Children."

So then Mum was OK when I went home. I was casual by then, wearing shirts and ties and trousers and all that. And instead of having short back and sides I started growing my hair a little bit longer and life got a lot easier for everything. For work, accommodation. You see, I always had a little feminine voice, that's what gave me away, my voice. I never spoke when I was out, never spoke publicly, I daren't speak because my voice would give me away. You were putting on this role and if you spoke, straight away they'd know you were a woman, so you couldn't speak. The young lads were the worst. They'd hear your voice and start shouting "fucking lesbian" or "queer" or something, so there was all that as well.

And toilets were a problem. You couldn't go to women's because if you went to women's they'd all come out screaming, and if you went in men's you had to go in a cubicle and if there wasn't a cubicle you'd have a problem as well. Toilet attendants would run you out as well, and going to buy sanitary towels, I had to get people to buy things like that for me.

COLIN:

My mother knew about it because I was asked to leave school but we never talked about it. I never said, for example, that Gerry was my boyfriend. People who lived in the same road as my mother used to say, "Who's that person your son always brings down at the weekend?" And she used to say, "That's my adopted son."

PETER B:

One night when I was fifteen I'd stayed out and come home with flowers thinking, "I'm in trouble now," and my father said, "I know what you've been up to, you've been associating with homosexuals." And I said, "Yes, so what?" And my mother said, "We've been expecting it for years."

I'd then left school and I'd started staying out at weekends and my father turned up one day and said, "You must come home now, your mother's worried sick." And on the bus going home he said, "I know what this is all about. I've been through all this and it never works."

But my father's homosexuality, in a funny sort of way, it didn't draw us closer together, it pushed us further and further apart, right up until the point when my mother died and I could finally talk to my father a little tiny bit and I used to send him gay fiction to read. He only outlived her by four months. My mother was a very nice person whose life I think had been ruined by marrying this man. He wasn't heterosexual, he was a gay man who had sex with women occasionally, probably twice – my sister and myself – and shouldn't have got married because he remained gay until the day he died.

I found it strange that my father and my grandfather were always arguing about performers and my father was always supporting pretty boy singers like, in those days, it was Cliff Richard, saying what a fabulous person he was, and this didn't quite seem the kind of thing he should be saying. He wasn't in the slightest bit interested in football or cricket. I was fifteen when my father made his admission and it wasn't really just until he died that I discovered that the reason he married my mother was on the rebound, because he'd been having an affair with her brother, who was killed in a motorcycle accident during the war. And then all sort of things fell into place because my maternal grandparents hated him and always said he was an evil man and my grandfather clearly knew what was what, having been in the navy in the First World War and having worked in musicals.

IAN:

My mother subliminally was pushing me into a gay lifestyle because she was afraid of losing me in a way. Very possessive woman. She didn't know it but any girl who I might be serious about, I usually got, "Oh that's not a very nice girl. God knows I want to see you married and settled down but I don't think she's the right one for you, Ian, I really don't." And the next minute I'd bring home a screamingly gay friend and she'd say, "Now that's a very nice friend you've got there." And I used to think, "Oh Mum! Do you realise what you're doing? You're pushing me towards all the gayest friends I've got and excluding any of the girls who I might be serious about."

JENNY:

Silly me, heeding the advice of problem pages in women's magazines to "tell your troubles to your mother". I did try this when I was about twenty, but she threw a total wobbly and said it couldn't be true and that I had to go and see a psychiatrist, blah blah, so I thought, "This isn't worth it." So I sort of pretended that it was a passing phase and I was over it now and no reference was made again, although she'd always get a dig in. If anyone was gay she'd say, "Disgusting, he's a pansy!" or, "Lesbians! How revolting!"

It was quite unfortunate to grow up with that, because if you were black or Welsh or Jewish, your parents actually know you're black or Welsh or Jewish, don't they? Both my parents were slightly right of Genghis Khan so there was nothing to be done or spoken about. My father died when I was forty-one and my mother when I was fifty-one but we never did have the conversation. I do think they maybe suspected because there were certain signs that I was not going to get married and I had "no sex appeal", according to them, because men just didn't come buzzing after me. My father said that I didn't have any boyfriends because I "ate too much garlic". Ha ha.

My poor mother didn't like children, period, like a lot of mothers in those days. So it wasn't really her fault, she couldn't help her feelings. But I always sought out older women until one day, when we were moving house after my father died, my mother read me out a letter from a friend of hers. She said this friend was "... so understanding. She always had an exact idea of what I felt, now listen to this. She says here, 'Well, darling, congratulations on your new baby.'" (This is not me, this is my little sister.) "'Let's hope you have better luck with this one because it must be so terrible to have a child like Jennifer.'" Then she tore it up and put it in the dustbin and I thought, "What's she trying to do?" I went completely cold because I couldn't believe she'd said that. I terribly wished I'd fished the letter out of the dustbin later on and stuck it together because nobody actually believes me. But I think it was because she had a child who was not in her own image, which I can now completely understand. She didn't get the dainty little daughter, she got this great stomping thing who climbed trees and wore dungarees. Now I do actually see that.

I then made up two children of my own, imaginary ones. One was very bright and never let you forget it. That sort of thing irritates me. And I gave her all the physical things I don't like, like buck teeth and bandy legs. The other was thick and dismal and wept all the time. I made them up because I wanted to understand how my mother felt about having a child not in your own image.

EMMANUEL:

I was at Bournemouth Arts School when my father died. He was fifty-six and this was an enormously emotional experience because I was so angry with him, daring to die. He died on my birthday. I felt that he cheated me of getting to know him and I was furious. So when I went to the funeral, I was furious with my mother for being so upset – and I cannot for the life of me work that out, it was totally illogical. She was just absolutely distraught over it and I just felt stony and hard and unfeeling and frozen. She gave me a picture of him when I was returning to college after Christmas and I ripped it up and threw it out of the railway window. I felt that it was partly because I could never tell him that I was gay, although I hadn't told myself by that time.

SUE:

I remember sitting around the table in the living room and saying to the kids that I had fallen in love with somebody else. Bill was six and he just cried and cried and cried. It was awful and Andrew, my oldest, he said to me, "Are you going to get married to someone else?"

And I said, "No, I'm in love with a woman."

And he said, "Oh good, you can't then 'cos two women don't get married."

They didn't want me to wear a lesbian badge to school. When they were eleven, twelve, they said, "Please don't wear those striped overalls and that lesbian badge you wear, Mum."

Bill has never spoken to me that much about it, but Andrew was kind of interested. I remember one evening, he would never go to sleep, from the age of about three he would stay up, the earliest he would go to sleep was about ten or eleven. I made him go up to his bed but he could listen to his radio. Anyway, one time he came haring down the stairs saying, "Mum, there's a programme about lesbians on now! Hurry, hurry!" So I had to race back upstairs with him and listen to some discussion about lesbianism.

I was out to my parents very quickly but they reacted terribly. My parents are Quakers but they were absolutely awful. My dad wrote me this long letter about how "Your mother and I will always love thee, but the idea of homosexuality has always revolted me."

He's come round now. He's fine. But my mum has never accepted it and she was terrible. She wrote to me immediately telling me that she was – big deal – disinheriting me and she was going to give everything she had to my husband. My mother said that when I wrote to him, "Your father cried. I've almost never seen him cry."

My dad said, "We request that thee doesn't tell thy brothers or our relatives." I wrote back that my brothers already knew – and my younger brother was gay and they never found out.

Where did they get it? I mean, the Quakers are really good! Why were they so bad about sexuality? My dad has come round to it but for years I would always have these fantasies of reconciliation with my mother, a great coming together of mother and daughter and we would tell each other things.

TAZ:
I came out to my sisters and they told my mum and dad. My sisters were wonderful, except for one, who was a doctor, who called me degenerate. My father said to my sister that if any brother or sister made any fun or treated me in any way differently he would not tolerate it. My lover used to come home and my mother even sent him off to pray with me once. But no problems there. I never went home without him.

BARBARA:
I had girlfriends and my mother and father used to accept them as woman friends of mine and I think in that generation, that was the Sixties, I think that's how the majority of people saw life. Unless it was actually thrust under their noses and someone said, "Do you realise?" It would never have occurred to them that there was ever any kind of sexual element in my relationships with women. If I had told my mother I think she would have said, "Oh, how interesting." That's how she was. Not my father though, he wouldn't have liked it, but he was Welsh, and of course all hell would have been let loose!

CYRIL:
I never told my family. My dad died anyway in '56 and I was only twenty-six and I was in a mess and didn't know where I was. Well, I did, but I was keeping it pushed down. I never told

my ma because she once said to me, "You're not a pansy, are you, Cyril?" Of all the words you could have used. That was Lancashire of course.

And I said, "No, no, I don't think so, Ma..." You know? Get off the subject?

Looking back, one was incredibly lonely, I suppose, and certainly in my late teens and early twenties I was getting all sorts of mysterious illnesses which I think was all to do with pushing it down and hiding it. And when you did meet someone you really fancied, not being able to turn to your parents and say, "Hey, isn't he fabulous? And I love him!"

REX:

In the late Sixties, whether it was before or after the '67 act came in, I can't remember, we were selling up my parents' cottage so they could go into sheltered accommodation, and I said to my partner, "Look, I'm going down," and he said, "Well, I won't come in because it's family business." So I drove down, went in. My brother was there with his wife, and my sister was there with her husband, and my mother poured out two cups of tea and I said, "John's not coming in." She said, "Why not?" And I said, "Well, this is family business." And she said, "He *is* family and don't you ever dare do that again." And if my mother said that, she meant it! I think it was absolutely wonderful to have parents like that, and they did treat John as a member of the family.

JEFFREY:

And when I eventually came out to my parents, which was in the early Seventies, after Gay Liberation, one of the things my father said to me was that he didn't mind what I did because he loved me and so on, but I wasn't to do it at home because there was always the danger of being caught, and he didn't want me to bring the family into disrepute. This was in South Wales in a mining village in the Rhondda, which of course was very constrained, very traditional in many ways, especially about scandal.

CYRIL:

As my nephews grew up I decided that I would tell them, each one, when they got to twenty, twenty-one, which was what I did. And the oldest one, Christopher, he came up to London because he was going to go to a further education college. He came up this particular Saturday, and I'd already told him I was gay, and he was going to stay at the YMCA. We came out of the station and on the opposite side was this young guy. I suddenly realised he was looking at me and actually giving me the eye and I thought, "Oh bugger." So we walked across and went into this student place that Chris was going to stay at, and as Christopher was signing in, this guy came in behind me and went up the stairs and sort of looked down at me and grinned. So Chris and I went up the stairs with his suitcase and I waited downstairs and he came down again and we had the rest of the day in London. I went to the theatre in the evening and then we got down to the tube station where he was going back to the YMCA and as he was getting on the tube, I said, "Now Christopher..." Oh yes, he'd already said to me that when he got into the dormitory, he said there was a guy there at the top of the stairs and he looked as if he was looking for somebody. So when he was getting into the tube I said, "If that guy you told me about is actually sharing your room," I said, "do be careful."

And he said, "OK, Cyril, or shall I give him your phone number?" And the doors closed and I just stood there!

IRENE:

I'm from Thailand. My Mum's a Thai and my father's Malay. I was married before for sixteen years to an English Jew and I came here in 1959. So we got married, my husband was in the air force, went to Richmond and then I settled in Twickenham.

I got divorced in 1981 and I came out as a lesbian in 1980.

I've got a daughter, she's forty-eight. The hardest task I had to face was to tell her that I'm a lesbian, but I was very lucky, she accepted and she was quite young. She is my hero. I first told her that I was gay and she went upstairs to her bedroom for about half an hour, so I went up afterwards and said to her, "Nothing's changed." If I embarrassed her, I wanted to do everything I could to help.

Then she went downstairs and she rang all her friends and told them, "My mother's a lesbian." So next day all the school friends came round to the house and had a look at me. So I said to one of her friends, "Why are you all here?" And they said, "We never see a live lesbian before."

I said to my daughter, "Why did you have to do that?" And she said, "Well if my friend doesn't accept you, they're not my friend." And that made me so proud.

Religion

VITO:
I'd never heard the word lesbian when I was growing up but I clearly knew my feelings towards women and I somehow knew I was different to some of my peers. I actually didn't 'practise', as it were, until I was about twenty-one. I had a religious bent in those days and I got confirmed in the church when I was seventeen and I really believed it was wrong, like so many people.

TAZ:
I was raised in a Muslim environment but it's only this late in my life that I've come out of the closet and said, "I'm a Muslim." I never met any other Muslims when I was involved in gay politics. It was a big major hole and as a result a very major part of my identity was submerged. A lot of people, when they come out, experience freedom in everything, but in fact I

traded one for the other, if you like. Before I couldn't say I was gay openly and I had my cultural environment, then I came out as gay and couldn't do my cultural thing because there was no room for it.

REX:
Around the time of the Montagu Case, through fear, my partner and I went along to All Saints Margaret Street, which is a very high church, and we got to know the vicar there, who said there was nothing wrong with being gay and in love with another man but you don't touch. We tried to live up to that, though it was a recipe for disaster, but you see you had on one hand the fear of the police and prison, and on the other hand, since both of us had religious upbringings, the fear of hell, and it was very frightening because the idea of a gay church was a long way away. But in his way he tried to support us, but he couldn't agree to two gay men being lovers. In love, but not lovers. So we were in a bit of a state.

6

COMING TOGETHER: THE BIRTH OF
THE LESBIAN AND GAY RIGHTS MOVEMENT

There is sometimes a discussion about whether it is general public opinion that advances greater social acceptance of marginalised groups, or whether acts passed in Parliament create a society which is more tolerant and understanding of a minority that has previously experienced discrimination. I see it as a chicken and egg scenario. Both are important, both can achieve an increase in civil rights and personal liberty. Examples can be seen, in Britain and in other countries, of cases where public opinion would undoubtedly never have changed without legislation; similarly, there are instances of reform in legislation that would never have happened without the influence of public opinion. But social and political advances relating to minority rights are almost always achieved when, at the same time, they are being spurred on by pressure asserted on a government by lobbying groups and political activists.

The 1960s and '70s saw a growth of gay and lesbian groups in Britain. I would like to give a general background here to when and why particular organisations developed. They were all committed in various ways to securing rights and creating environments where, for the first time, gay men and lesbians could gather freely and discuss issues around their lifestyles and their sexual orientation.

The Homosexual Law Reform Society was founded in 1958 by A.E. Dyson, who also set up the Albany Trust (the charity arm of that organisation) to provide support to those "suffering from intolerance, persecution and social injustice". The main aim of the Homosexual Law Reform Society was to lobby Parliament, and Antony Grey (whose real name was Anthony Edgar Gartside Wright), a barrister and a journalist, was the society's main and best-known lobbyist.

CHE (the Committee for Homosexual Equality) was formed in 1969. It became a national organisation and attracted support from leading figures in the medical profession and the arts, together with some from the church. In 1971 it changed its name to the Campaign for Homosexual Equality. As shown in many of the following memories its emphasis was seen by some members as being less on political agitation and more on creating social networks and possibilities for lesbians and gay men to meet one another. Jenny tells us: *"We used to get these edicts from head office about how we ought to be campaigning for this and that and marching and so on, but we just used to have fun and parties and dances, get to know each other and just be happy as a group."*

In early July of 1969, due in large part to the Stonewall riots in June, discussions in the gay community in New York led to the formation of the Gay Liberation Front. One of the GLF's first acts was to organise a march in response to Stonewall, and to demand an end to the persecution of homosexuals. Aubrey Walter and Bob Mellor then founded the British branch of the Gay Liberation Front in London, on 13 October 1970 at the London School of Economics (LSE), where Mellor was a student. GLF made the first-ever public demonstration in the UK by lesbians and gay men, at Highbury Fields, Islington, to protest the use of 'pretty policemen' *agents provocateurs* to entrap gay men into attempting acts of gross indecency. A media group was established which produced the GLF newspaper *Come Together*, which ran to sixteen editions. An anti-psychiatry group was formed with specific focus on the use of electric shock / emetic drug programmes on gays and lesbians. Also formed were a women's group, a street theatre group, a communes group, and the youth group for the under twenty-ones, fighting for a reduction in the age of consent.[1]

Several of the contributors to this book were participants in the meetings and activities of GLF and I find it particularly exciting to hear their personal recollections and impressions of those seminal events. Mary tells us that she and her girlfriend *"... were in the anti-psychiatry group and we were in the manifesto group that wrote the GLF manifesto and we did an issue of the magazine,* Come Together*".*

Jeffrey attended the Highbury Fields demo and says: *"Much more exciting for me than whether we were challenging the police, was the fact that we were all there together, we got a high from that. And in fact that was the night I got off with Angus, my first long-term partner, so it had lots of other excitement."* Other contributors, such as Taz, Bob and Emmanuel, also give us personal insights into their involvement in GLF as well as their hopes for, and occasional disappointments in, that relatively short-lived but historically significant political movement.

This chapter concentrates on predominantly male-led reform groups, although we do hear from Mary about the women's split from GLF. But the next chapter will concentrate in greater detail on women's groups, politics and concerns around lesbian rights.

CS

~

Interviews

The Albany Trust and the Homosexual Reform Society

GRIFF:

I knew about the Albany Trust and the Homosexual Law Reform Society because they used to take out a small ad in the *New Statesman* about once a month. The Albany Trust met at 32 Shaftesbury Avenue. I think Antony Grey was the queen bee, or whatever. He was a writer on legal matters but I think he became involved realising that the cases he was having to handle, the law, was so cruel, and it should never have been, but he would preside at these meetings. There was always full attendance, about a hundred and fifty people, and then we'd go round the corner to the pub, The Crown. Antony Grey would say at the end: "We'll adjourn now and continue over a drink in the pub."

There was a lady called Marion who worked at the Oxford University's British National Bibliography. She'd come in at lunchtime to do the records, and take the membership of the subscribers in the Albany Trust. When she'd seen you there a couple of times, you were safe and she'd ask you back to her soirée. Once a month, I think it was the first Wednesday of the month, in a bedsit at the top of the terrace in Ladbroke Grove, round there. You'd climb all these stairs, one room, and there'd be about fifty gay men in there at any one time, just chatting and drinking. You'd bring your own drink and you'd sit there for half an hour or so, and during the course of that Wednesday evening there'd be about a hundred and fifty gay men traipsing in and out, and there you'd meet policemen who were gay. This would be '64, '65. At Marion's it would be exchanging information about which coffee bar had opened or if something had happened and the police had visited one, that type of thing, you'd get the intelligence. And people in the Albany Trust wanted to do things so we formed discussion groups and we'd meet fortnightly, usually in somebody's house or flat, and we'd do things like addressing the envelopes for the CHE or Albany Trust mailout or letter to the MPs. Their phraseology and their charity status, their aims and objects, was to provide for the wellbeing of a minority. I don't think they used the word 'homosexual' at all.

RON & ROGER

Ron: We were in the Homosexual Reform Society.

Roger: That was the precursor to Stonewall. I forget the man's name now.

Ron: Grey. Antony Grey and some friends. That wasn't his real name.

Roger: But again, it was illegal. They were walking a tightrope. I think they were people in, shall we say, the upper echelons, the upper class. They were an important organisation.

Ron: We got certain booklets which gave guidance on what to do if you were arrested. It was like a survival kit.

CHE

JENNY:
I got involved with CHE, Campaign for Homosexual Equality. Snore title. There were groups all over the place and we joined and it was quite political. But ours was in Kensington and we were quite frivolous because we thought that people ought to get to know each other and feel comfortable before we started marching about with banners and lobbying our MPs and that sort of thing, because it was a long time ago and it was not done to be queer at all.

CHE was quite a nationwide organisation. We used to get these edicts from head office about how we ought to be campaigning for this and that and marching and so on, but we just used to have fun and parties and dances, get to know each other and just be happy as a group. Because 'gay' was a really bad thing to be then and a lot of people were very neurotic and frightened. Frightened mainly. And people would creep into the meetings and want to die and you'd want to be nice to them.

We used to have the meetings in a pub. Our leader was a school teacher and he told the publican that we were a group of homosexuals and then they wouldn't let us have the room. We also had a poetry group and we'd learnt from the pub experience not to say we were gay so when we went to hire another pub for our poetry group and they said, "What's this all about, then?" our inspired schoolteacher said, "Oh, we're called the Company of Nine." Because we were nine poofs or lesbians who'd come together to read poetry. So as the Company of Nine we had a wonderful time in this pub in Floral Street, doing poetry programmes. We actually did poetry readings and meetings and everybody used to organise an evening, on a theme usually, and get others to read. I never managed an evening though and I would never read because I'm too shy, but I didn't half enjoy the events. My job was to do the tape recordings. I was all right with that.

The gay men and the gay women all really enjoyed each other. Most of us girls didn't really like men that much, because heterosexual men are a dead loss as they're only nice to pretty girls and if you're not pretty, forget it; and the poofs didn't like women very much either. But then we all met up together and we found that we really got on. I've got friends to this day that I've had from all those years back. We had a lovely time. They really were fun days.

Through CHE one met a broader base than with *Sappho*, the lesbian magazine. We used to have outings and picnics and God knows what. Once we all gathered for a picnic in Hyde Park and everybody brought their own grub and there were about forty of us having this sort of mass picnic, it was really good fun. We hired films and showed them in the library in Kensington Town Hall and we'd have Mae West and that sort of stuff. Of course we told them we were a film group, we didn't say we were poofs. We had learnt after that first experience, because we really did feel that we were the worst people in the world and you had to be so careful who you mentioned it to.

We used to go to Speakers' Corner on behalf of CHE and Jackie Forster bravely climbed a ladder and said, "You're looking at a roaring lesbian!" And people would heckle and throw bricks and so on. She talked about legal rights and how they shouldn't be shoved under a carpet and how there were many more of us than they thought and how they were probably all around you. And funny little people would sidle up afterwards, 'cos we used to have little bits of paper saying, "Go to a CHE meeting in Something Something Street." So we were actually out doing that, holding the banner saying, "We Are Lesbians," and of course the first time we took the banner out we didn't know you had to cut holes in it, and we were blown all over Hyde Park.

SHARLEY:

In the late Sixties, the Campaign for Homosexual Equality was basically people campaigning around decriminalisation of homosexuality and I was also into campaigning and I kept writing letters to the press. In those days that was all you could do really. So I found out about CHE and I joined that and became a campaign secretary for one of the groups and was very involved with campaigning. In the beginning there was quite a strong lesbian group, but at one of the conferences lesbians felt that gay men weren't giving them enough space and didn't really understand about lesbians and they broke away, and I just felt one had to get at gay men to make them understand. The group I belonged to were really very nice people and we became friends, so I stayed with CHE, which caused a bit of an upset at the time. I really felt that one could do quite a bit inside.

CHE has been superseded by Stonewall, but in the old days we really did campaign. I can remember going to a boiler-makers' union and talking about homosexuality. The mind boggles now. They were all men and some of the cleaners had come along. We did things that were really quite dangerous in retrospect, like going to that boiler-makers' union, because we knew we would get a very hostile reception but we didn't care.

Speaking at Speakers' Corner in those days was pretty horrendous. Jackie Forster was also doing that but we started our own platform, CHE, in 1976/7 and that was really quite something. And the heckling! You were made aware you couldn't possibly go on your own because you'd be attacked. I've been chased in the underpass of Marble Arch tube station. But somehow one wasn't really afraid. I can remember one time I was chased and a young man caught up with me, a soldier who had been heckling me all afternoon. He'd really been vicious and I thought, "Oh gosh," but he said he wanted to apologise for his behaviour but he was gay and because he was with his mates he had to be extra nasty in case they suspected him of being gay. You had people coming up to you who said thank you for coming out here and speaking. People from abroad thinking, "This is fantastic, there's a gay and lesbian platform here." So that was the positive side. I enjoyed that. I really did.

I can remember we had formed a London group at CHE and when Ken Livingstone was first installed at County Hall, GLC, we wrote and to our surprise we were invited and doors were suddenly opened. It was the most exhilarating experience. I can remember going up to the County Hall and we were given a room and you had a lesbian group, you had a gay men's group, and you suddenly felt you were not being ignored, you were somebody, that people understood about sexuality – and that was very, very liberating.

TAZ:

All I remember was my first meeting was in the Holborn Assembly Rooms, I think, and I'd gone along and they were trying to construct a letter to MPs or whatever about being homosexual and the legal system and all that. And while people were standing there waxing lyrical and extremely elegantly using Greek classical analogies and everything else there was, I was sitting there being a fundamental, basic, honest, salt-of-the-earth queer.

I think the most instrumental speech for me was listening to Jackie Forster when she first stood there as a woman at Speakers' Corner. Because CHE used to do Sunday afternoons, getting speakers to stand at Speakers' Corner, getting people to speak to the public, and I couldn't believe it when she stood up there and said, "I am Jackie Forster. I am a lesbian."

I thought "Oh my God!" And everyone stopped dead in their tracks. She handled the heckling and everything else beautifully, beautifully, and I was so thrilled and I felt so proud, you know, that it, I suppose, galvanised me in that way, in some respect, and particularly when she could claim to be a mother and she had been married and there she was saying, "I'm a lesbian."

And also it was the first time I'd seen anyone deal with those kind of insults. Because as an Asian, and it's still one of the problems today, to stand outside in public and say it, because the abuse you can get is just so fundamental and basic, that I thought, "Well, wow, if she can do it..."

EMMANUEL:
We became members of the local CHE group and became quite active in it. I'd moved to Finsbury Park and the group was North London and the people were interesting and I made one or two friends and we held what we thought was the first meeting on homosexuality at the library, which was just next door to Holloway Prison.

Gay Left

EMMANUEL:
In CHE I met people who'd been in GLF and there was still the rump of something called the Gay Marxist Group. At this point I'd become terribly interested in politics and we then started going to that group and formed a new group which was called Gay Left. That was around 1975 and that was infinitely more interesting. It was formed of quite high-powered intellectuals. It didn't have an aim. CHE was a social group with a political purpose for law reform and equality in more areas and for a lot of men, they joined and it was really a means of meeting other men to get sex basically, they didn't really want to get involved in the activities. But in this group, the Gay Left Group, there was just about six, seven or eight of us and we had a very specific agenda which was to look at the relationship between sex and politics, Freud and Marx; the way of Marx as a political philosophy and the way of Freud as a means of understanding ourselves. And we read

Freud and Marx, and had discussions about it. We looked at topical issues which might include issues such as paedophilia, cottaging, dance and so on.

Gay Liberation Front

JEFFREY:
For me, getting involved in Gay Liberation transformed everything. It formed in 1970 and I was in London. I was actually working at the LSE where the first meetings were held, so I learnt about it through flyers on tables. I couldn't go to the first few meetings, I went to the third and fourth I think, and it was revelatory in all sorts of ways because I'd been in bars lots of times but here were a hundred people plus, and groups of many more than that later on, all there, open about their gayness, women and men together. Different ages, sizes, degrees of prettiness, ugliness or whatever and we were all there together and that was tremendously liberating, amazingly liberating. But it did more than that because Gay Liberation was also a political movement, so politically it radicalised me, and thirdly, I met my first long-term lover there who I was with for the next ten years and I stayed friends with until he died. So it was like a personal transformation, a political transformation, a cultural transformation, all at once.

One of the things that GLF wanted to do in London was actually display that we were there and challenge authority to say no. We had dances in Camden Town Hall, in Kensington Town Hall, various large venues. The very first demonstration of GLF was at the end of November of 1970. That was after a then-prominent Young Liberal activist, Louis Eaks, was arrested for having sex on Highbury Fields and somebody at a GLF meeting, I think it was Antony Grey actually, suggested that we ought to demonstrate about this. So about forty, fifty of us gathered on Highbury Fields on a Friday and had a torch-lit procession protesting against police harassment. I don't have any memory of whether there were any policemen there but there was a reporter from *The Times*, which was our first bit of publicity.

Much more exciting for me than whether we were challenging the police, was the fact that we were all there together, we got a high from that. In fact that was the night I got off with Angus, my first long-term partner, so it had lots of other excitement. And on the tube going home, on the Victoria line from Highbury and Islington, we all crowded in and we started kissing and cuddling in the carriages, to the bemusement of those sitting there.

We did a number of demos in the early days; one was outside The Gateways in Earls Court, the famous lesbian bar which existed through the Sixties. Some of the women who used to go there, Mary McIntosh, Elizabeth Wilson and others, had been kicked out for distributing leaflets about a Gay Liberation meeting, and so they announced this at a GLF meeting, and we decided to demonstrate outside The Gateways, led by women but a large number of men were there as well.

Gay Liberation had been going on in the States for a year by the time we started in London, so there had been a little publicity about it but not a huge amount, and then it erupted in London. It was a small movement at this stage, I mean, we're talking about a few score of people, perhaps a hundred people going to meetings, and often lots of the things we did, as in the Gateways thing, were directed at our own community.

CYRIL:

In GLF there were the guys with frocks who were causing a lot of consternation among the general population. They were outrageous and people were complaining about them but in fact if it hadn't been for the Gay Liberation lot we wouldn't have got as far and as quickly as we did. They were mavericks and we were all terribly buttoned up. "Don't rock the boat, let's do it quietly, we don't want to alienate people." But they just came out and literally were just wearing outrageous clothes and screaming, "Gay Pride!" and we were all going, "Ssshhh."

MARY:

My girlfriend and I joined GLF together. I'd heard about it from a friend of mine called Roy Bailey who's now a full-time folk singer, but at that time he was a lecturer of sociology. He was one of those gay men who only had one-night stands, this was in the late Sixties, and he and I were both involved in something called the Deviancy Symposium and he said, "Some people at LSE have come back from America and they're starting a Gay Liberation Front." And we sort of gulped. We'd heard about Women's Liberation and we thought, "They're trying to model themselves on Women's Liberation," and we thought, "Yes!" Because it fitted everything that certainly I'd been thinking and writing about at the time.

We went along to the second meeting but we then started being conscious of the fact that it was quite male and we set up a women's group so that that would give us strength and so forth. So Elizabeth Wilson and I went to the second meeting of that when it was still quite small, I mean there were about twenty or thirty people in the second meeting. At the third meeting there were, I don't know, about fifty to eighty, and then it started meeting in the big old lecture theatre at LSE and by then there were hundreds of people. It was so exciting, it was just absolutely amazing!

Both Elizabeth and I talked quite a lot at meetings, so a lot of the men would have known us, just because we got up and talked, whereas some of the women, they didn't talk so much. It had a lot of subgroups. We were in the anti-psychiatry group and we were in the manifesto group that wrote the GLF manifesto and we did an issue of the magazine, *Come Together*. There was a big split which was always characterised as the women leaving GLF but it was a bit more complicated than that. One of the people who'd started it was Aubrey and Aubrey's boyfriend was Dave Fernbach who was a '68 LSE student leader, so he was sort of a political heavy.

Someone wrote an article called 'Gayness and Imperialism' or something like that, or 'Gay Oppression and Imperialism', I can't remember what, which was an attempt to link gay oppression and Gay Liberation with anti-imperialism. So the article was submitted to the GLF publication, *Come Together*, and David didn't want it published. Before that it had had a very open... it had had lots of different points of view, so the *Come Together* collective split about that and that split came to the main meeting. It was quite complicated because a lot of the women wouldn't agree with it but they didn't like David and those heavies saying it couldn't be published, and it was a bit odd because Elizabeth and I were kind of much more left-wing than most of the women and we were quite interested in the content of the article, at least in the linking of the two issues. But David, by that stage, had turned against trying to do a Marxist analysis of gay oppression and he didn't want anything to do with that – and his main reason was that he wanted to be a kind of populist leader within GLF. This is what I think, anyway, and he knew that all the queens would think that all Marxism stuff was so much rubbish, which is quite true.

So the women left over this and we left basically because David and Aubrey, to some extent, were steamrollering their position and their leadership of the queens over us and wouldn't listen to us when we said that we thought that some of the radical drag was oppressive to women and so on, because radical drag was the populist thing. I think David even tried to wear drag on one occasion, which is not his thing at all! And we said, "Hang on, what are these images of women that you're doing?" They were doing things like frumpy women, with, you know, stockings and handbags and that kind of thing? And we said, "What's going on here?" and they didn't seem to know any other way of doing drag other than that, or kind of high camp. We sometimes thought that they didn't have much of an understanding of the politics of it.

I actually didn't agree. I mean, there was kind of a radical feminist strand which I didn't agree with because I thought that what those blokes were doing was quite political, they were exploring different ways of doing drag that weren't about high heels and make-up and nail varnish and all of that and I thought that was actually quite interesting, what they were doing, but they didn't ever consult women about it and I thought they ought to have done.

So it's very odd how those things developed. They're partly about personalities and power struggles rather than just about issues, but when the women left, the whole thing started to fall apart and people started setting up local groups. It was much too big and it had almost no structure to it so it was very easy for it to collapse.

NIC:

I'd been involved with GLF but less so as there were splits about those men not being interested in women's issues. There was a split between some feminist approaches and also about the age of consent. There were issues about them wanting a lower age of consent, much lower, for boys, and that caused a massive row because age of consent affects everyone, girls too. There wasn't much awareness of power relationships so there were lots of arguments that had gone on. I mean, throughout my political career I suppose I've never been a complete separatist. I've had moments of nearly being, but the gay men's fight has been where it's converged and we've worked together.

TAZ:

With GLF they were talking more about things that were to do with my day-to-day existence as a gay person, whereas CHE had grander plans. They were involved with political lobbying and so on and, looking back, I now realise that it was a class thing. CHE was extremely upper and middle class. Gay Liberation seemed to be ordinary hippy types and young people trying to find their way and their identity, and political identity too. There would look at things like lifestyles, how do people live? I ended up becoming associated with a gay commune which was set up through GLF. When I was first taken to it, it was in Bounds Green and then it moved around. It started, I think, as a squat, and then moved into legitimate rental. In

GLF all of a sudden you felt you were connected to a network, so people would say, "If you go to anywhere else, we've got connections in this country or that one." In America there were gay organisations you could ring up. GLF always had a list of crash pads. No matter who came to London they could ring up and say, "Is there anywhere I can stay with gay people?" People just volunteered their places as crash pads, including this commune, so the aspect of being connected to a wider community was very much with the GLF.

In the commune we had wonderful times! Of course there was a lot of recreational drug use going on at that time. The commune was very politicised, all gay issues, race issues. Everyone was right out there doing something or another, anti-apartheid movements, anti-Vietnam, trade union movements, etc. It was extremely aware in that way and politically active. People actually did participate and join resistance groups or whatever, so it was a different form of political activism compared to CHE, which was a much more status quo way of dealing with issues. It was to do with respectability and GLF appeared to be too 'out there' because we discussed things like gender issues, what was then called 'gender fucking', which was blokes dressing up in drag, which I did as well, make-up, the lot, just go out there and be; because we were trying to challenge the given stereotypical ideas of gender, sexuality etc.

There were demonstrations that were organised. The first gay demo was wonderful. They were very large, you know? They started small but they then gathered a huge crowd around them. There were always people round there and the most amazing thing was when we had a mass 'kiss-in'. I couldn't believe it because we were all tonguing each other and everything, in the middle of the public, as a protest. We also used to do it on demonstrations. Somebody would say: "Now! Everybody have a kiss!" We kissed in public because you weren't allowed to. This was around 1972, '73.

But the political activities of GLF, they were looking at different ways of organising, consulting, getting consensus, it was extremely experimental and challenging and vibrant. You were always encountering ideas, literature, performance art, the whole gamut. But it didn't quite attract the serious respect that it should have at that time.

EMMANUEL:

I went to one or two of the early GLF meetings. They were all mixed up with lots of different things. I found them enormously exciting and enormously threatening, because what they wanted was something that was totally out and totally confrontational. I felt that this really put my life in jeopardy because I wanted them separate and they said, "No, it shouldn't be separate." It was terrifying and I think I really found that very difficult to cope with.

The GLF became terribly marginalised very quickly. It was an idea and right from the very start it set up two groups of people who took it forward, they became interested in Marxist ideas and they set up the Gay Marxist Group and they produced pamphlets. I don't know how long they held public meetings, but I don't think there were very many and they were a bit scary.

BOB H:

In those days, '71, '72, it was a sort of a clubby, pubby scene. It tended to be drag cabaret acts in pubs and then just slightly after that the first discos started on a Monday night at venues that wouldn't otherwise have anyone in them and then that happy little 'in the closet in the week, out at weekends, back in the closet again' was all slightly shattered. I can remember quite distinctly, sometime in 1971, '72, somewhere about then, possibly a little bit later, as we came out of our Sunday night at The Union Tavern, our last fling of the weekend before work again, and these peculiar people from the Gay Liberation Front were outside handing out leaflets saying, "Stand up for your rights. Come out. Be counted." And we always thought, "Oh gosh, what's all this about?" We thought they were lunatics and very inconvenient. We didn't want to come out and stand up for our rights! We didn't want to be outed and the rest of it, who would want to do that? We were just interested in partying. So I remember that quite distinctly but also feeling guilty because I thought they had a point actually, you know? If we're all in the closet how's stuff going to move forward? 'Cos it was like a secret society in those times, you did things on the quiet.

BOB C:
I joined GLF in 1971. I came back to London from Tanzania where I was doing VSO and not long after that the Gay Liberation Front set up. I was living in a flat near Notting Hill Gate and one of the places where GLF met in the early days was in a church hall in All Saints Road and I had heard about it and I just decided to go along and give it a go. My first experience of being with black people was them running their own country and Tanzania was quite a good place to be, in comparison with some of the other places I could have been sent. That really politicised me so I was very involved in anti-apartheid politics when I came back to London and I was quite open to the Gay Liberation Front and its politics.

I wasn't part of it in the very first year when there were the splits between radical fairies and all the rest of it. My experience was just of being part of a bigger mass of mostly gay men and some gay women so it was quite good in that I didn't get involved in political infighting. It was just like a good place to find my way around and to get to know people. I joined a consciousness raising group and there were about eight of us, used to meet every week for about six months or so just to talk about ourselves and what it meant to be gay. It wasn't a group where we had sex with one another, it really was a group where we just came and talked. There was a weekly meeting of GLF at this church hall which anyone could go to and I tried to go along to that most Wednesdays and there were lots of kind of zap things which I was too scared of to take part in. I remember them zapping W.H. Smith for some publication they

Ron and Roger in Chicago in 1962 (above, Ron on left); and in London
celebrating 50 years together (Roger on left)

Ossie (left) and Peggy on a motorhome trip through the Rockies, 2005

Sue at her 40th birthday party in 1981

Mary (above, right) with fellow activists Jackie Forster (left) and Doris Lerner at Pride in London's Brockwell Park in 1995 for the 25th anniversary of the founding of the Gay Liberation Front (photo by Nellie Pollard of GLF)

Vito (left) and Valerie at Pride, 2008; and Vito in her Wrens uniform

Jack recently and in his younger days

Left: Jenny as a little girl

Below: Susan on a cruise to celebrate her 70th birthday

Alex (right) and Ian on St Martin's Lane, London, days after they met, early 1960s

Peter B, early 1970s

Rex, c. 1950

Bob C on a demonstration in 1975 and (right) at Brighton Pride in 2011

Sharley being 'sainted' on her 70th birthday under the Hyde Park Gays and Sapphics banner

were selling, and people would dress up outrageously and go into somewhere like Smith's and make a protest against some publication. It was more dressed up rather than actual drag.

There was one incident about going to the Imperial College bar and I think there were about twelve of them, six men dressed up as women and six women dressed up as men, and they went to this bar that refused to serve women and it completely blew the minds of the bar staff, because they didn't know who to serve and who not to serve. And although I didn't take part in that kind of street theatre, I was influenced by it and I thought it was wonderful, really. There were also incidents where people would go into gay bars that were not very friendly towards GLF and demand to be served. There would be sort of respectable middle-class gentlemen in there drinking and then all these student types, radical fairies, would come in and rock the boat. I was too scared to join in but I do remember being in a bar once when these people from GLF arrived and I was delighted to see them there.

GLF became very big and then it just crumbled and they tried to set up local groups. There were different tendencies, like south London were really into radical drag and a lot of the men there would wear women's clothing, not like drag queens but a 'gender fuck' kind of attitude and they did develop in quite different ways.

7

SAPPHIC LIFELINES: LESBIAN GROUPS
AND THE WOMEN'S MOVEMENT

I could quite happily write and edit an entire book of recollections devoted solely to the issues covered in this chapter. During the 1970s and '80s, women in western society, both gay and straight, publicly, politically, academically and personally examined issues around their sexuality and sexual identity in greater depth than had ever been seen before, or very possibly since.

Many issues, events and ideologies to do with both feminism and lesbianism are addressed and discussed in this chapter and so, in this introduction, I will give a little supporting background. Several of the women who have given their stories played crucial roles in forming and shaping lesbian groups and politics during the time span that this book covers (1940s to 1990s). With regard to some of the very first lesbian groups that are mentioned, it emerges from the contributors' extracts that there was sometimes a fine line between whether women were seeking and joining these groups for social or political reasons. Maybe it was a bit of both. But some women, I am sure, whatever their initial motives, probably had very little idea of how politically and historically important their activities would be in heralding the dawn of a society in which lesbians can now enjoy a previously unimagined degree of legal and social freedom.

The Minorities Research Group was co-founded in 1963 by Esme Langley and Diana Chapman, making them the first women to bring lesbianism into the arena of public debate. Carol remembers Esme as being *"a very butch woman, a bit like Radclyffe Hall, very upper class as well"*. And Jenny recalls her time working as an illustrator on the group's magazine, which was called *Arena Three*. She explains how the publication *"... ended up being* Sappho *magazine when Jackie Forster took over* Arena Three *and it got relaunched."*

Ros refers to Kenric as *"my lifeline"*. Kenric was established in 1965 for socialising and that particular organisation continues to this day to provide a network of social groups for lesbians around the country.

Norma talks about her experiences of being the only black woman at Sappho, and at the OLN (Older Lesbian Network) – which was formed in 1984 with a grant, as she tells us, from the GLC (Greater London Council). The GLC played a huge part in allowing lesbian groups to exist throughout the 1980s. Under Ken Livingstone, who was elected to be the council's leader following the Labour Party's GLC victory in May 1981, the GLC became the focus of the labour movement's support for gay rights.

The London Lesbian and Gay Centre (LLGC) was a community centre established in 1985 and paid for largely by the GLC. These premises provided a vitally important space for LGB groups to form, meet and socialise. Even though the Eighties was politically a Thatcherite era, lesbian and gay groups in London, in particular, because of Livingstone and the GLC, were able to form and indeed flourish with public funding in a way that had not been seen before.

Although their sexual orientation had not been legislated against in the way gay men's had, lesbians lived (and still live) in a patriarchy. So, when the feminism movement gained significant ground in the Seventies, it was only natural that lesbians would endeavour to find a political voice within that movement and begin the slow process of raising awareness of issues around their own sexuality and lesbian visibility. I personally feel that there is a certain irony in the fact that discussion around lesbian politics appears to be less prevalent now than it was when we were working and marching alongside our heterosexual feminist sisters several decades ago. One reason for this may be that because straight women are desired sexually by straight men (who will pay more attention to their feminist views and demands than those of lesbians), the level of discussion about lesbian matters within the feminist movement could not help but become marginalised after heterosexual women gained a certain amount of ground politically and personally.

But still this period saw the politicisation of many women and at times lesbians could even be seen as taking over the feminist agenda, for example, in the case of Greenham. In 1981 a women's peace camp was set up just outside the fence surrounding RAF Greenham Common airbase with the intention of challenging, by debate, the decision to site ninety-six Cruise nuclear missiles there. Tens of thousands of women either lived at, or visited, Greenham Common airbase up until the year 2000, when the camp was finally brought to a close. Women began to choose to live at Greenham because there they could be at the cutting edge of protest, and lead a life apart from men. As they did so, a culture of lesbian 'separatism' became dominant.[1]

Spare Rib was a publication set up in 1972 to provide a feminist alternative to the conventional women's magazines. Contributors Susan and Sue held various positions there and Sue very candidly tells us: *"Working there [...] was dramatic and intense. Don't let me slide over the fact that it was hideous as well. It destroyed people. I mean, all of the fights that we had there were so destructive."*

But despite such problems, *Spare Rib* provided a lifeline for many women, for whom it was sometimes the only means of contact with the Women's Liberation Movement (WLM) and emerging feminist thought. As the British Library website describes: "The movement was built around networks of local women's groups and national conferences where representatives from those local groups could meet for strategic discussion. It established networks for support, analysed women's roles and relationships in society and defined a set of demands for the social and economic equality of women."[2]

Several groups and campaigns mentioned in this chapter include both straight and lesbian women acting politically in a common feminist cause. The Reclaim the Night marches started in the UK in the 1970s. Around that time, a man who would go on to become known as the Yorkshire Ripper was murdering women, some of whom were prostitutes. Feminists in the area were angry that the police reaction to these murders was slow and that the press barely reported on them. The police advised all women not to go out at night, which angered the feminists, as well as a variety of women's and student groups. So they organised a resistance of torch-lit marches and demonstrations, and they walked in their hundreds through the city streets at night to highlight the fact that they should be able to walk anywhere and they should not be blamed or restricted because of male violence.

The marches continue to the present day because, as the London Feminist Network argues, "women are still blamed for rape and male violence".[3]

Gill remembers certain Reclaim the Night marches and events and comments that, *"What was so interesting about Reclaim the Night was that it was such a creative way of demonstrating."* She and Linda also refer to being involved in certain WAVAW activities. WAVAW stood for Women Against Violence Against Women and throughout the late 1970s and early 1980s the group focused on educational campaigns to raise awareness of what they viewed as the harms caused by pornography and the sex industry.

Also in this chapter, references are made to consciousness raising (CR) groups, which had first started in the United States and allowed feminists to gain a better understanding of women's oppression by getting together in local groups to discuss and analyse their lives.

Jean and Susan give stories relating to their personal experiences of lesbian custody cases. There is a view that whilst lesbianism was never actually made illegal, legal discrimination against lesbians in this country has historically taken more circular routes to achieve its aim, for example in laws relating to child custody.[4] The Rights of Women Lesbian Custody Group was formed in 1982 to campaign and research around the difficulties lesbian mothers faced in retaining custody of their children. They noted that whilst very few lesbian custody cases were actually heard about (which they put down to the fact that lesbians were advised by the legal profession that they stood no chance of gaining custody through the courts), in a number of cases that did go to court, the judges made openly moral statements about their views on lesbianism which suggested that, rather than considering the best interests of the child, they were more concerned with controlling the moral behaviour of society.[5] This information serves to highlight just how courageous and groundbreaking the custody cases fought by women such as Jean and Susan were at the time.

CS

~

Interviews

Minorities Research Group, Arena Three and Sappho

CAROL:

I was in London after I split up with my girlfriend and I thought, "What can I do?" And I got some publication, I think it was called *IT*, *International Times*, it was a bit like *Time Out*, and I saw this advert saying, "Are you a homosexual?" And it was the Minorities Research Group, they were a charity and they had publications with helplines and you could write to them. So I wrote them a letter saying how I felt so down with myself and that I would love to meet people and they recommended *Arena Three*, which was the very first gay women's publication. So every month they'd send you a little magazine – in a brown envelope, of course, so your parents or anyone couldn't see it – and it had little adverts in it and stuff and I met two gay women who I got on with. One lived in Surbiton, she was an artist and I love painting so we wrote to each other for about six months; and then I wrote to another one who lived not very far away and I went to meet her. Barking Station. Went to her house for tea. Very butch. And as I was leaving a man came into the room in a wheelchair, it was her husband. I nearly died!

Arena Three was great. That was Esme Langley. I knew her. She was a very butch woman, a bit like Radclyffe Hall, very upper class as well. Plenty of money, had a big house off Chelsea and we all went round giving her ideas how to set it up in the early days. And then she set up *Arena Three* and that was before *Sappho* started and all the other women's stuff and it was brilliant because it had lots of contacts, lots of political stuff as well and topical things. I wrote a couple of articles about Ford's women who were fighting for equality at the time – they didn't get it and they had strikes and all sorts of stuff and they did eventually get the equal pay with the men. But it had a cookery thing and gardening, an old-fashioned *Diva*, if you like. But that was all we had, so I met a few people through there.

JENNY:
My girlfriend Marion and I heard about *Arena Three*, the magazine. It was started by a woman called Esme Langley and it ended up being *Sappho* magazine when Jackie Forster took over. She called for volunteers, one of which I was, and I was put in charge of subscriptions (now we've leapt into the Seventies by the way) and we ran that from her front room in Connaught Square and it did pretty well for several years.

I got to know Jackie because *Arena Three* had an advertisement for a film showing in Selby's Dining Rooms, which is where Marion and I had first met when it was a Jewish function room. We decided to go to this film because it was one somebody had made for television about gay women. So along we went and Jackie Forster was the chairperson and was with her then girlfriend, Babs Todd, and we thought, "Umm, we like them, let's see what we can do for the magazine," sort of thing. So Marion just said, "Is there anything we can do for your magazine, because I'm a journalist and my friend Jenny here is a photographer?"

We weren't a bit political. We wanted to meet other lesbians because we hadn't really met any, other than those really heavy dykes. We wanted to meet someone that you could walk down the street with and if you bumped into your mother you wouldn't have to run away and hide. And Babs and Jackie looked like perfectly normal women and they were obviously very articulate. So we volunteered our services and yes, Marion got co-opted into writing a monthly column and yes, I took photographs, or did illustrations if it seemed more apt. I also took over the subscriptions department, making sure everyone got their magazines every month. Of course they wouldn't take our adverts in papers like the *Observer* or *The Times*, but we got a few in *Time Out* and gradually, I think, some of the big papers let us in, and it had quite a good circulation. We brought it up from about three subscribers to really quite a lot of people.

And why was it called *Arena Three*? Something to do with the folding of the paper, I think. It was A3 size or something. That was definitely the first lesbian magazine. You felt that you were doing some good. People would write in saying, "I think I'm the only one in Biggleswade," or wherever. We also used to go to Speakers' Corner. Jackie was very brave. She used to be Jacqueline Mackenzie. She was pretty famous in her day and had her own television show. She was extremely funny and very clever and we all miss her a lot.

SHARLEY:
I met a lot of really nice people at Sappho and I knew Jackie quite well. There was a degree of snobbery there from professional women, which I resented a bit. When you were a nurse you weren't really professional, you weren't a doctor or a lawyer or a journalist. But on the whole I got on really well with Jackie and we were very supportive of each other. I was very careful about alcohol and I didn't smoke and they did not like that. It was weird that my lack of drinking offended them. I realised that just because one is a lesbian, one doesn't necessarily get on with every lesbian one meets. That it's just as diverse a group of people as heterosexuals.

They had speakers at Sappho. It was often very Women's Lib, often general perceptions of sexuality, lesbianism in general, the way the press reported on lesbians. The only person I really remember, I can't even remember what she talked about, was

Katherine Whitehorn, when she worked for the *Observer*. She's not gay but she was very positive.

SARAH:
I met Jackie Forster at Sappho, it was at Reeves in Shepherds Bush. Very exciting, very nice to be with those women at last. There were talks by different people, there was one by the Whiplash lady, the one that ran the brothel, Linda somebody. I missed that talk and there was Pam St Clement who gave a talk at The Victoria and then some lady came and talked about how you shouldn't have relationships between Jewish people and Christians.

Jackie was a very tough and charming woman and I sometimes wonder if these young girls who openly walk about holding hands feeling very free... whether they realise what this woman did, how she paved the way. It was a very difficult time in the 1950s.

CAROL:
There was The Sols Arms in Camden which was a pub and Jackie Forster did a Thursday night for the Sappho women, but they were a bit boring because they were talks and lectures, political things. Jackie was very political and she'd have some good speakers but I didn't like to sit around, I liked to have a dance, have a drink and have a laugh, so I weren't that into that.

NORMA:
So the next thing you know I started buying magazines. I think there was one called *Gay News* and I'd buy them and look for any gay events. I saw this Sappho meeting and went along. It used to be upstairs in a pub in Ladbroke Grove and I found it. I walked around and I think I must have gone in the bar downstairs and asked somebody and they said, "I think you

want upstairs." Jesus! Good job I'm black or they would have seen me blushing! That was back in 1979. There were loads of women there and I didn't know what to do or what to say. It was a bit lonely. I think I was the only black woman there and that happened such a lot in lots of places that I went to.

Sappho had a magazine at the time which I think I bought at the meeting. Jackie Forster was there. She seemed frightfully middle class and I thought, "Oh my God!" But as it turned out it was all right because I met her several times after that and she always recognised me and was always very friendly. Jackie and somebody called Geraldine ran Sappho. It was all new to me so I learned as I went along. They had things like Married Women's Night every second Tuesday and I thought, "What does this mean?" There were people describing what they identified as, some were saying 'lesbian', 'bisexual', and all that. I thought I must be bisexual because I've had relationships with men, I've had children, so I said 'bisexual', you know? But after a while I realised you don't say that in a lesbian setting!

ROS:
A friend of mine called Eileen Dixon was on the committee of Sappho and so my girlfriend and I started going to Sappho. It was a discussion group and I remember one woman sitting there knitting a jumper and I thought, "Do I really want this?" But the discussions overran that. They were about everything, everything! They used to have people come in and give a talk about sexuality or lesbianism, maybe films, books. That was held in a variety of places but the main one was held in Bayswater Road. Jackie Forster used to run that 'cos she was on the committee. I loved Jackie, she was ace, she was brilliant. When I look back, she was like an icon to us younger ones because she was so confident and she knew everybody and everybody knew her – and a lot of people liked her, put it that way. She could be a little bit... abrupt sometimes, but generally she was lovely.

Kenric

ROS:

I first came to London when I was twenty-three, so that was 1969/1970. I rang up Lesbian Line and they told me about Kenric. So I went along to the boat trip which they used to have on the Thames and they had two queues going into the boat, one at the front and one at the back and I was in one of them and I was looking round and I thought, "I'm at the wrong place, because there's men here." And I was talking to a girl and I said, "Is this Kenric?" and she said, "Yes."

I said, "Oh fine." I said, "What about those people over there?"

And she said, "Oh yes, they're Kenric members."

And I went, "But they're..."

And then I realised that they were girls dressed up in all their gear. But they did look like men to me.

I was frightened because I didn't know anybody and it was the first thing I'd ever been to. But I felt comfortable, they were very friendly. Then I was sitting there and there was water around my feet. I think I was more worried about the water round my feet than I was about the women. So that was the first ever thing I went to. The chairperson of Kenric was Rita Mendoza and many people remember Rita, she was fabulous. She used to greet everybody with her sailor's hat on and her outfit, she used to wear the sailor's hat and ribbons down the back and made everybody feel welcome.

I will never, ever thank Kenric enough. I mean, that's why I do so much work for them now. They were my lifeline because when I rang up Lesbian Line, I was just so, well I'm not a depressive person, but I was socialising, but in the straight world. And the girlfriends that I was socialising with, there was one of them that I fancied or maybe two of them and I thought, "This is ridiculous, why can't I meet people like me and then if I fancy them then it's all right. I'd be safe then." And that's what I did. But we used to go to lots of Kenric dos. In those days we used to have the conference room at the zoo, the big ballroom, and there'd be a thousand people there. But it was non-political and I'm not a political person so it's sort of as if it was made for me.

Spare Rib

SUE:

I joined *Spare Rib* in 1979. Before that I was on this journal called *Red Rag* that wasn't solely lesbian either, it was a socialist feminist journal. So the job in *Spare Rib* came up and I'd loved being on *Red Rag* and all the other little publishing stuff I'd done so I just decided to apply and I got it.

Spare Rib was absolutely fantastic. I've never had an experience like *Spare Rib*. Being part of the Women's Liberation Movement sent me spinning and then becoming a lesbian I spun up even higher, then joining *Spare Rib* was just amazing. But I can remember taking the train from Farringdon on my first day, on the way home, thinking, "I'll never learn how to do this." I didn't know how to do proper layout and I'd never even seen proofs in the way they came back from the typesetter. You know, these great long scrolls you had to proof? You had to do all this cutting out. It wasn't like now. You used scalpels and marked the proofs with blue pencils on the side and I thought, "I don't know what I'm doing!" So learning all that was really wonderful. I love the production of magazines. Love it. And I would just think about it all the time. It captivated me. The idea of a monthly publication and how it would all fit together. Planning articles in advance. I loved all of the collective meetings we had. I just loved them and I wrote stuff as well. I even edited a book called *The Spare Rib Health Reader*.

There were about ten or twelve women working there and it was dramatic and intense. Don't let me slide over the fact that it was hideous as well. It destroyed people. I mean, all of the fights that we had there were so destructive, fights about anti-Semitism and Zionism, fights about racism, fights about lesbianism, fights about class. Those were the main ones. The conflicts were real but the way we fought was so destructive.

Spare Rib was never apart from the women's movement. We were sitting in this building, putting out this magazine. We were part of the Women's Liberation Movement. Looking back it's absolutely clear that we could be nothing but reflective of everything that was going on in the women's movement as a whole. But at the time we would be held accountable all the time and we would feel that we should be held accountable, whereas now we'd probably say, "Fuck off, if you don't like it. It's just our point of view!" But then we got "How dare you?" from different women and groups. So you'd publish an article and then you'd get a group saying, "You got it wrong. You have to print a retraction. We have to have an article in the next issue. We demand a meeting." So many issues became divisive and often, within the collective, we'd have these very complicated and many-layered tensions, tears, screaming, running out of the office.

When I came in '79, *Spare Rib* was probably about half lesbians and half straight women and then it got to be a few more lesbians. There was a split when we had an article from a woman who made accusations that the magazine's content was too lesbian and that lesbians excluded straight women and so we had this discussion about how to deal with articles that could be seen as anti-lesbian. There was a feeling around that it was just too painful and too horrible for lesbians to have any sort of attack or any kind of negative stuff aimed at them. But myself, and a few other women who were lesbians, we argued that we all had to learn how to fight, to be in the real world, and that you didn't combat anti-lesbianism, sexism, racism, by banning it, you had to engage with it. And to engage with it you had to open up the pages of the magazine to discussion, otherwise you would just be shoving it under the carpet. So we had these endless things with questions like "Do we give a platform to a racist?" Well no, we don't. And we don't give a platform to avowed homophobes. But if somebody, as a woman, was saying, "I feel you're excluding me and lesbians are taking over," then we wanted to openly struggle with her and have articles and debates about that and for lesbians to be able to say, "This kind of accusation makes us feel this way and anyway, what makes you, when it's completely not the case that lesbians are taking over the magazine, feel that way?" I think the whole women's movement was going through these tensions and I think it's because lesbianism was challenging accepted norms in lots of previously heterosexually dominated groups.

SUSAN:

Well, I suppose my happiest years as a lesbian were at *Spare Rib*. When I first joined, I think it was 1976, the collective was on the change, opening up to a wider range of women, whereas before it had been that group of quite wealthy Oxford and Cambridge educated women. I think it was set up in about 1972 but when I joined it was branching out and they were looking for new blood. A friend said to me, "Why don't you come on the *Spare Rib* collective?" And I said, "Well, I don't know if I know enough. I do identify as a feminist but I don't really know about the National Abortion Campaign" – and all the issues that I imagined were happening – and she said, "Oh you'll soon pick it up."

So I went to work there and I was one of a collective of about ten women. We were in this crumby old office in Clerkenwell. We all did everything, so I was one of the editors. What I actually did was a lot of commissioning articles. I did a lot of editing, a lot of co-writing, a lot of ghosting.

I identified strongly as a lesbian there and there were women of different sexualities there and dabblers, which was not OK in those days. You were very suspicious of bisexual women in those days and heterosexual women, it was like a completely different world. I felt a bit intellectually outclassed and I felt a little bit of a social class outcast because some of them were also quite upper class and middle class and I felt that I didn't really know as much as they did, which was the truth, about Women's Aid, NAC, and those nitty-gritty socialist feminist activities and commitments.

But I did identify as a socialist feminist and once I went to *Spare Rib* I got more interested in radical revolutionary feminism, because they were more lesbian-centred and I found it very hard to understand how the socialist feminists would have such strong bonds with men because I became quite clear that men were the enemy. But I had to be quite careful because a lot of my socialist feminist friends were strong lesbian and they were very sure that class was the main oppression and not patriarchy. So we got really involved in these debates all the time and for the first time in my life I had a diary. It was the antithesis of being a hippy. There were millions of meetings on all the time. Millions of demos.

STEPH:

I was very interested in feminism, in fact I've got some old *Spare Ribs* and they're quite fascinating. There's a lot of articles that are very similar to things now. I was really interested but I was put off by what I saw as the disapproval of boys because I had two sons. If there was an event you could have gone to with your children, they didn't really want boys to go to it, and so therefore I thought, "Well, how can I go?" Also I didn't think that was a very good stance to take, because you should be influencing the boys as children, so no point excluding them. All I felt was that they're not welcome, so therefore I can't get involved because I don't have anyone to leave them with. So if I'd have had two girls instead of two boys I think I would have done a lot of things differently.

Women's Liberation Movement

SHARLEY:

This was in the days of Women's Lib and *Spare Rib* and people doing consciousness raising and women's history, so you got involved with all those groups. There were other campaigns like Ban the Bomb and there was the hippy era and among the hippies there were so many lesbians and gays, you met them on the street. We had straight friends who politically agreed with us. They weren't anti-lesbian, or anti-gay as it was in those days – 'lesbian' was coined much later. Lesbians said we were ignored under the word 'gay'. We had started the Hyde Park Gays, we had a platform there. We got a lot of stick because we just called ourselves Hyde Park Gays so I added "and Sapphics", which was a good move because the number of people who would come up and ask, "What does Sapphic mean?", and you would then explain.

CAROL:
The feminism thing was quite big in those days, late Sixties, early Seventies, and there was a lot of straight women jumping on the bandwagon, wanting to be gay because they thought that being a feminist should go with being gay. Half the feminists were straight and had children, but it was a political thing to do, to be gay at that time, so you had to be very careful who you were with.

My girlfriends always wore lipstick, so you'd go somewhere and you'd be butch but you wouldn't be like her, she'd be in her lipstick and her hair and all the rest of it and these feminist types, supposedly gay women, would come up to her and say, "Why are you wearing lipstick? Why are you wearing perfume, stockings and shoes?" So you'd have problems with them like that. So we didn't really gel with them, we had problems with them because they didn't accept us the way we were, 'cos if a girl wants to wear lipstick she's entitled to wear lipstick. But they were straight women themselves really. So we weren't that keen on them lot.

EMMANUEL:
A group of lesbians set up Lesbian Left and in our group, Gay Left, as men, we were often held up for criticism by politicised lesbians for not including women, but there were no women to include when we started. So they set up their own group and lots of lesbians became lesbians through a political rather than

a sexual channel and lots of the women who became lesbian reverted back to being heterosexual.

We had a meeting which was hideous. We knew lots of individual women in the group who were very nice but as soon as they got together they tended to be terribly critical and really wanted to destroy Gay Left because it didn't have women in it but also because they were terribly anti-men, for no reason that we could understand. I'm sure that they could understand it. We published a magazine called *Gay Left* for five years and a lot of them wrote for that, they contributed to it.

Although as gay men and lesbians we shared lots in common and lots of differences, the lesbians were split by lots of different factions; one was the political lesbian and one was the life lesbian / the desire lesbian and this was a big split, and indeed how do you resolve that?

And lesbians had never been illegal, not that that makes life any easier for a lesbian than for a gay man because we all suffer. I think that the same social stigma is there, maybe worse for a woman.

MARY:
When the women left GLF, the whole thing started to fall apart, but we had already started moving towards Women's Liberation and before the split we went to a Women's Liberation conference where we were able to talk about the whole issue of women and sexuality. At that stage the women's movement was going through a whole change, and we were the catalysts for that. From 1972 I went to national conferences which saw the beginnings of the socialist feminists, but in '71 and '72 onwards lots of women who were joining Women's Liberation with heterosexual histories were thinking that the way forward was separatism; that lesbian relationships were the thing to do – and heaps of them did have lesbian relationships, so you were at the cutting edge at that stage.

What happened in the Seventies was so interesting, when so many women were able to become lesbians that hadn't been able to before. But for some of the political lesbians it was just what they thought they ought to do.

LINDA:

I was in the Labour Party, I was the leader of the Lambeth Council and of course I was in a number of lesbian groups, but in those days, in the early Eighties, the Women's Liberation Movement was effectively falling apart. It fell apart due to loads of issues: Israel's invasion of the Lebanon and the kind of fallout of whether you were deemed a Zionist or not and then S&M was another area that caused the Women's Liberation Movement to fall apart, where we started getting dress codes.

I was living in Brighton at the time and I remember a National Abortion Campaign meeting. When I went to the meeting I was very conscious of how many lesbians were present and none of us made any issue about being lesbians because we could only talk about abortion from a heterosexual point of view, from a women's point of view. So it really kind of galvanised our consciousness around being lesbian as distinct from being a feminist.

I loved the Women's Liberation Movement and I hated it. It was a kind of huge umbrella. There were seven demands of the Women's Liberation Movement and lesbians were the last one. It was about recognising lesbian rights but it began to split the movement. This was the late Seventies. So my sisters in the WLM were encouraged to keep their sexuality to themselves because we might frighten the horses.

When I joined the movement I was one of many assertive lesbians who were saying: "Come on! A woman's right to choose is not just about abortion, it's about everything." I wanted to be the whole of me. At least I had the benefit of a black consciousness in the sense that we'd fought for the right to assert ourselves in our culture, so why couldn't I be a lesbian?

I was active in a number of lesbian groups and the CR group I was in, I was out as a lesbian. The CR group was Women Against Violence Against Women. We met at AWP, A Woman's

Place, which is now a police station just off the Charing Cross Road. It was an old building which was squatted and it was run as a collective with no funding. There were newsletters which would notify you of the events and activities going on. There'd be a meeting about this, there'd be a social, all kinds of things. It was extraordinary. The thing about the women's movement was that it was autonomous groups. As long as you subscribed to the principles of Women's Liberation then you could be recognised.

Then there was the Women's Arts Alliance, which was another hotbed of lesbians, at Regents Park, and events would go on there. There would be a Saturday night event, it might be poetry reading, it might be somebody playing dreadful dirgy music. It could be all kinds of things but it was creativity and we used the Drill Hall as a venue. Every night in Islington or central London there would be a different lesbian event or a social activity going on.

I was involved in Angry Women. A few women agreed that we would have a number of national events. We targeted *The Postman Always Rings Twice* because it was a film that showed violence against women and we co-ordinated a day which we made known through the network. So a number of Angry Women in Leeds and Brighton and elsewhere organised a number of events to protest against violence against women. 'Some' people made eggs which were put in an eggbox and they were filled with paint and they were thrown onto the screens of the cinemas. 'Some' women went into a cinema and got up at a certain point and pelted the screen with these eggs with black dye in and then said some words and left the cinema and then did something similar to sex shops, and every woman had to make sure that there would be no risk to life. So you may not target a sex shop where people live above or next door if it might have jeopardised them, even if it was them who were legally responsible for the sex shops. We would not have risked life.

There were other things that we did. I remember – not because it was desperately illegal, it was just annoying to W.H. Smith –

but we would get lots of porn from the top shelves and go along to the checkout and then refuse to pay for it. We'd stand and argue about what this disgusting stuff was. So we disrupted the shop.

GILL:

If I remember, I'm trying to think back, we had a march in Lewisham and I think what had happened was there had been a couple of, I'm not sure if they were murders or rapes, a couple of atrocities but the reason we were so incensed was that the advice was that women shouldn't go out. "You shouldn't go out." And you can see now with hindsight that that's probably very sensible but it came over as "You've got to stay indoors," rather than "We're going to go out and find these men," which was probably, as I say, sensible, but you got the impression that they were blaming the victims rather than going after the men. I mean, you probably wouldn't go out, but you don't want that being put over as being the police's main response to the fact that, I think it was two or three women, had been brutally murdered or assaulted in South East London.

So, as a result of that, if my memory serves me right, that was where we got Reclaim the Night. We're not going to be told we're going to stay indoors; actually we're going to be out there. I remember a Reclaim the Night march in Lewisham, I think it was maybe 1980, in a place called Studio Seven, Lewisham, which was a cinema which showed some sleazy films. The other incident was when, as a lawyer, I represented a woman who was prosecuted for throwing paintballs at a cinema showing. I think it was possibly a Brian De Palma; he made those sort of slasher films in the Eighties, and they were paint-bombed. There was a big spate of paint-bombing. What actually happened was I got this call that this woman had been arrested and would I phone the police station to find out what was happening? So I spoke to the station sergeant who said, "Isn't it funny how you type always know what's happening." There was all this suspicion about being a lawyer and you must have been part of it and whatever. But those were the words, I remember it to this day, "Isn't it funny how you lot always know what's happening." In fact I didn't, I had no idea and I wouldn't have wanted to know because it was criminal damage and in fact a lot of damage was caused to the screen because if you damage those screens it costs a lot of money to replace them. So I think the woman was caught because she had red paint on her hair and on her hands.

But of course the other thing we had in South East London were these things called Private Shops, I don't know if they still exist, but basically they were shops selling pornography and they were in the high street and they would have blacked-out windows. They popped up in suburban areas and I remember there was a spate of women supergluing the locks to these shops. It worked! Cost them hundreds of pounds to get into the shops again.

Around about the Reclaim the Night stuff, somebody designed a poster to put over the Pretty Polly posters and I think it was 'Polly Rapist' or something. So women would do things like they'd go into the tube and they'd stick posters over those sorts of posters. So there was that, which was very creative, and graffitiing, that was another thing that happened. What was so interesting about Reclaim the Night was that it was such a creative way of demonstrating. I remember when I was in my first women's group in 1971, two things stand out that got a lot of publicity: one was that they occupied the Wimpy Bar in Park Lane or wherever it was, because they wouldn't serve women after midnight because they were prostitutes. I didn't do that but the other one I was on, we did lots of stuff around abortion clinics and there were only about ten of us but like with the Wimpy Bar all the women dressed up in their finery, like streetwalkers, walked in and wouldn't leave. They were really interesting things that were very creative.

Then of course they all disintegrated in the Eighties when you had the Lesbian Strength marches because the lesbians wouldn't go anywhere near the Gay Pride marches and they wouldn't go on a march with men. I actually do remember women were being asked to leave because they were wearing combat jackets and they were thought to be militaristic. I mean it all got absurd. It was all around those politics of "You don't really look at who the enemy is, you just kick the person next to you as it's easier", whether it's class or race or anything, so you got a lot of policing of who could do what. It was really horrible. But if you look at that period, during the Eighties, I think the separatists did have a disproportionate influence on politics for women, they really did. I look back now and I remember one of my clients who'd left her male children, that was not unusual, or a woman who had builders in and didn't feel she could reclaim the space that the men had been in.

I remember being in WAVAW, Women Against Violence Against Women, which politically wasn't really where I was, but I remember that we were talking about child abuse and we were basically told that we were nutty because "Oh it couldn't really be on that scale, because you're paranoid". And then Esther Rantzen comes along, sets up Childline and people then accept that there's this terrible child abuse going on, sexual abuse – and that happened because she had acceptance, respectability, she was not seen as man-hating.

NIC:
A lot of women had been in GLF and CHE and other things. I mean, I'm not talking about a homogenous group of women, they'd all been involved in different politics that I knew so you couldn't say 'our journey'. I would say there were many journeys. I would say that some of my friends were socialist feminist, some were revolutionary feminists, some were radical feminists, you know? They all had a different history.

SUE:
I used to dress up a lot more with women than I did with men. There was the butch/femme thing happening and I just sort of did it and liked it and then later on when it got very prescriptive, you weren't supposed to do it – all the Sheila Jeffreys kind of

stuff. I've met women much younger than me who really felt they were being denounced if they were into butch/femme, and most of all if they were seen to be femme. But I never really felt that and I think that was because I thought if it's lesbian feminism, I've been a feminist for a million years, nobody's going to tell me what to do! I felt like I belonged. It was *my* movement and nobody was going to tell me that I couldn't do stuff. I was that much older. I'd been around.

Greenham Common

LINDA:
I didn't go to Greenham on principle because I didn't see it as part of the feminist struggle; part of the human struggle but not part of the feminist struggle. If they'd said it was a universal struggle, I would have been there.

GILL:
Greenham didn't challenge state power; it was all this stupid holding hands around a bloody fence. What was that going to do to overthrow capitalists? Mine was a quite masculine idea about it. I was a socialist but I was still mixing with some of this radical revolutionary feminist stuff so I was not politically in their camp but still doing things with them. I knew quite a lot of women who were radical revolutionary feminists but we didn't think men were the enemy, we thought it was class.

Lesbian Custody Cases

JEAN:
When I first met Mary, I fell in love with her immediately. I was married and my daughter, Frankie, was three. I knew I had to tell my husband about it sooner or later because I couldn't live a lie so I told him that I'd slept with this woman. He seemed OK

at first and because he was quite an intelligent man I thought that we could work it out, but then he started beating me up. He was a big guy, ex–rugby league player, so I'd go to school with a broken nose. Twice that happened. He dead-legged me so I couldn't walk. Threw me through the front window once. So eventually I had to leave because I knew it was affecting Frankie. There was no way he was going to let me have her. I mean, he named her after him.

I drank a lot to be honest but I didn't miss a day's work at school. At one point he wouldn't let me see Frankie for eight months and then out of the blue he called me up and said I could pick her up from school that day and have her for one night. That was so difficult, after all that time, and when she was eight he said he was filing for divorce.

I knew Jackie Forster very well and so she recommended these solicitors in Gray's Inn Road. They were very expensive and very good but they didn't see at that particular time how I could win custody of Frankie. The solicitors had advised me that probably it was best just to go for joint custody, and I would have to continue paying maintenance, which I had been doing voluntarily, so it was very hard. Frank was there, telling lies, but I just kept quiet. They said to me, "Are you happy for him to have care and control?" I didn't say anything and that was it. It was actually over in half an hour. The decision was that we had joint custody. He had care and control and I was to have access and that was to be arranged. I paid the top rate maintenance. I did ask Frankie, she was about ten, what she wanted to do, which is hard, asking a child. But he put a lot of pressure on her. He said that she was his little wife, his little woman, that he couldn't live without her, and so it was easier for her, I think, though I don't know now, that I let him have care and control.

This was the late Seventies. There weren't many women who won custody of their children then and there was a lot of anti-lesbian stuff in the press. So I missed out on all Frankie's childhood and her teenage years. I saw her once a week and I've never had her at Christmas. It's just lost time that you can never make up.

SUSAN:

I went through divorce proceedings with my husband and I suppose, as an out and open lesbian, I was famous for being one of the first women who went through a custody case, but without any feminist legal support. My custody case went on from when my daughter was three to when she was sixteen. You never got once-and-for-always custody, it would keep coming back to court. It was agonising to have that passionate love for my daughter when every two weeks she would go off with my ex-husband and we'd never know if we were going to see her again, and I would never know if he'd get custody or skip the country. I was a teacher when it all happened, but my husband, every time he found out I'd got a new job in a school, he'd write to the head teachers. But of course they were all lesbians! So they would just call me in and say, "We've had this letter..." So that little device of his didn't work. So in 1970 the divorce came through and I got custody, care and control. But then it never died a death because every now and then he'd think, "I know, I'll get back at Susan, and I'll take it to a new judge," because there just weren't any other openly lesbian mothers around. That didn't start for several years later.

OLN

NORMA:

There were some women's centres which I used to go to a lot and then there was one in Acton and I met a woman there who said to me, "There's this thing for older women on Saturday, do you want to go?" So I went along with her and that's when I joined OLN. They met on one Saturday every month. It was at Archway then, and I just kept going. They had workshops and things. You'd bring lunch to share and then split up into workshops and have discussions about whatever subject anybody wanted to name, about relationships, about sexuality, about lesbians with children, they always had a political one in those days as well.

The grant that got OLN started was from the GLC, it came out of a conference. This was 1984. There used to be an older feminist one and I think the lesbians wanted one for lesbians, so they got this grant. I went along there and for years and years I was the only black woman. Occasionally someone might put their head around the door, maybe an Indian or mixed-race person. I remember going for about three months and I felt quite isolated. There were one or two people that tried to be friendly and I think it was about the fourth meeting, I thought, "This is going to be my last because I don't think I can cope with this." They always announced before the end what they were going to do afterwards, like they might be going to The Angel or whatever, but nobody actually said, "Do you want to come?" So I probably went home. Then somebody said that once. I remember this woman said would I like to come back to her place with some other women? And then we became friends for a while and I thought, "OK, things are looking better, maybe I'll keep coming back." And it did get better.

I was grateful to OLN because I thought, "At least there are some other lesbians here. They may not be black, but at least they're lesbians so I'll keep going." And it did me well. There was a time when I would not do anything on an OLN Saturday: "Don't ask me because I'm not available!"

8

LESBIANS AND GAY MEN IN MARRIAGES AND COMING OUT LATE

Bob L makes it quite clear that when people like himself were younger there were very few credible alternatives for opting out of marriage. *"Anyone aspiring in any profession had to be married. You were very odd if you didn't marry."* He tells us, *"I was engaged twice because that was how one could conform and then hope it would go away."*

Some gay men were referred to as 'not the marrying kind' and some women escaped for a few years or even decades into the armed services, where there was at least a possibility of avoiding questions about their marriage plans. On the whole, though, people who are now between sixty and ninety years old saw no alternative but to marry when they were young. Consequently, several of the interviewees in this book have been married and some of those have had children. Certain contributors, even if they did get wed, felt that they were not suited to marriage but did not understand why that was so. Sharley tells us that after seeing a psychiatrist who told her that she was a "homosexual woman" she thought, *"How on earth can I be, I'm married? But then I thought she maybe confirmed something which I realised within me. It took time to get used to."*

Several older lesbians I know have told me that when they were young they wanted to have children and that getting married was the only way open to them to do that, whereas nowadays, of course, there are far more possibilities for lesbian and gay couples to have or to adopt children.

Some of the interviewees have said that they had relationships with both men and women. As we all know, sexuality can indeed be a fluid state where people don't always like to define themselves as one thing or another. But just because someone talks about their marriage and maybe their children, and then later – or even at the time they were married – about having same-sex relationships, we cannot automatically assume that they are, or were, bisexual.

As we saw in the first chapter of this book, several of the contributors said that they wouldn't have called themselves 'gay' because they didn't know the word. So I would suppose that, similarly, few would have identified with the term 'bisexual' at a time when the word was rarely used. Jack is the only interviewee who describes his going out with men and women when he was younger as having a *"totally bisexual attitude"* but interestingly enough, no other contributors used the term 'bisexual', even the ones who were married and having same-sex relationships at the time and those who came out as gay or lesbian later in their lives.

Nowadays there are terms within the sexuality spectrum that people can try on for size to see if they feel comfortable adopting and identifying as them, but from the 1940s to the 1980s people did not have the luxury of choosing a name for their varying sexual identities.

In that era, people who had sex with both men and women could have been doing so because they couldn't fully accept their true sexual identity and felt it needed to be mitigated or seen as somehow redeemable. Jack says, *"I don't know whether I was setting out to prove something by dating women or whether it was the time that we were all growing up in."*

Perhaps they thought of themselves as bisexual because they didn't want to admit, even to themselves, that they were completely gay, or maybe it was a way of keeping a door ajar through which they might one day leave their unaccepted 'gayness' behind. Or it may, of course, have been the absolute truth.

CS

~

Interviews

SARAH:

I had lots of young men who were after me and I was just so bored and this man eventually became my husband. I thought he was such a rock and a wonderful guy and I married in 1959, very happily I might say. I was twenty-nine, a bit late. Then I had two children and went to live in New York. I gave up everything to do with the theatre. It was marvellous living in New York in those days and I concentrated on the children but there was always this thing, niggling me, leaving me mentally on my own. Then we moved from New York to Germany. My husband was a specialist lawyer in the Common Market. He was just a lovely guy. He didn't speak an awful lot. English rugger player, you know? The very antithesis of what I really needed, which was just a lovely woman. Then when we went to live in Lubeck we thought we needed some help with the children and this au pair girl who was about nineteen came over. She was there with me for about a year and a half and I just wanted her so badly.

She used to have her day off and and one day she came back and said to me, "I think I go mad." I said, "What's the matter, Nicola?" She said, "Last night I slept with my girlfriend and a Chinese man."

We had this farmhouse and we were in the garden underneath this plum tree and I said to her, "Nicola, you slept with your girlfriend? Why not me?" It took some courage, I can tell you.

So she said, "What, you? In your position?"

I said, "What position? What are you talking about?" I said, "I'll see you in my room tonight about eleven o'clock."

I put the candles on and perfume on the bedspread, it was positively medieval really, and that was like falling through stars. Then we got completely hooked on each other and that was difficult and I used to get out of bed with my husband and go in with her. I didn't have any conscience about it, I really didn't. I'm sure it was wrong to be married and do that but I did it anyway.

Then I came back to London thoroughly bored. I went to live in Wapping and I used to steal away at night because my husband didn't like dancing and I used to go to The Gateways Club and that was fun. And then I met this man called Louis in that place in Earls Court, The Coleherne. I saw these bright blue eyes looking at me and he came up to me and said, "Would you come out with me?" And I said, "Yes I'd love to," and we went out for years together dancing. We used to go to Napoleon's, just off Bond Street. It was about five floors of gay men. He was a wonderful dancer and I loved dancing too. We went to the Prince of Prussia, or whatever it was called, where they all wear these Nazi uniforms. Little tiny men, some of them were, and they all had their uniforms.

They didn't talk to each other, they were standing up against the walls sort of looking and they had their leather trousers, it was very strange, and Louis used to say, "Ooh, see that one over there? I really fancy him. Would you go over and talk to him?" So I'd go up to the guy and say, "Where do you come from? My friend really fancies you." And then I'd go back to Louis and say, "Yes it's OK," and he'd say, "Oh don't bother, I don't fancy him anyway."

So after that I moved to Dorset and I'd been there for a year and a half and my husband died quite suddenly and this gay friend of mine said, "I know it's tragic, but you're liberated now." I know, but what a way to be liberated!

SHARLEY:
I was probably a late developer sexually and then so many other things happened, that feeling got pushed to the background because other things became more important in a way. I married, because I'm German by birth, I was here during the war and it was said we'd all be repatriated to Germany. So by marrying an Englishman in those days you automatically became English and to me that was, at that time, of prime importance.

I was a nurse and we had a lot of nurses who were lesbians, probably closeted, and there was just one couple who we realised were lesbians and I could understand that, felt akin to them. In marriage I found the sex life absolutely disgusting but it's not because I was prudish or anything but just my husband touching me really gave me the shivers and I was so upset that I eventually tried to commit suicide. It so happened that the doctor who came referred me to the Tavistock Clinic and I saw a psychiatrist who told me that I was a lesbian. Well, actually she said, "You're a homosexual woman." She didn't use the word 'lesbian' as far as I remember. That would be 1949, maybe 1950. I didn't believe her. I thought, "How on earth can I be, I'm married?" But then I thought she maybe confirmed something which I realised within me. It took time to get used to.

I tried to find out things from libraries but there was absolutely nothing. There wasn't a gay switchboard, there wasn't a lesbian line, there was nothing. My husband was a ballet dancer and he was with a company and I knew there were gay men in the company and basically in the beginning just talking to one of them helped me tremendously, even though he knew very little about lesbians. But he then introduced me to other gay men and it was basically being in a political group that I met another lesbian.

A friend of mine had found out about what they called a Knitting Circle in Notting Hill Gate and it was just lesbians and most of them were married. A couple of them were in a relationship together, but it was marvellous. We called it that because it was in somebody's home. She was married and her husband was away regularly but that's where we met. It was fantastic. We had a really lovely time, it was total relaxation. It was just what we called ourselves. And through that I joined the Women's Liberation Group.

This woman lived in Arundel Gardens in Notting Hill Gate and once a fortnight her husband wasn't around. She had a lesbian friend, partner really, and there was nowhere to meet at all. She went to Gateways and spread the word that she was going to have a meeting in her home. They would have to call it something very simple, they hadn't come up with a name then and apparently with the first lot of women who turned up, her husband returned early and he said, "What's this then? A knitting circle?" And that's how it got its name. They said, "Yes, we're looking at patterns." Of course they didn't have any wool or anything, but she made sure after that that there was wool around.

It went on for years. It was really nice because it was informal. You brought tea to share, biscuits or whatever, and you had a jolly good natter. You could cuddle each other if you wanted to and it was very, very liberating. It wasn't oppressive. What was nice about it was that there was nobody with a strong ego complex who wanted to run things. It was fantastic, it really was. You more or less had to tell her you wanted to come and sometimes she'd ring you and sometimes she'd say, "I'm sorry, we're going to be full up." You could fit fourteen people into her space and that was crammed, but usually there were fourteen people there and if you were a regular you got preferential treatment anyway, if she liked you. It was her flat but we all helped with the clearing up. It would start at three o'clock and it would go on till about seven o'clock, every other week, and I used to make sure I got time off. It was really good, very, very pleasant. There were occasions when she managed to get rid of her husband at weekends and she'd let us know if anyone wanted to come this Saturday or whatever. You could really relax.

BOB L:
I was engaged twice because that was how one could conform and then hope it would go away or, in many cases, now I know people who hoped they'd be lucky in that nobody would find out about their other life. Anyone aspiring in any profession or anything had to be married. You were very odd if you didn't marry and the obvious reason was that you were a confirmed bachelor. I'm very glad I didn't marry because I would have hated to be the cause, especially if I'd had children, to be the

cause of any break-up or heartache for any partners or children involved.

As it happens, a number of people I've known, people my age now, who did marry, they've seemed to come through quite well in later life. Many of them have been open with their families and have been accepted; not everybody, but a lot of them have. Partly because that side of marriage is over now, especially the penetration part, you can be just good friends now. So now they've reached a certain stage where people can be more open once they've taken that step of saying things and they finally tend to accept, as far as I can see.

SUE:

I came out very late in life. I must have been in my mid thirties. I was active in the Women's Liberation Movement and I remember that lots of people were beginning to come out. There were the beginnings of Gay Liberation and of a lesbian presence. I mean, there were a lot of lesbians around anyway but it was gathering speed, if you like, and I remember thinking to myself, "That's for people who don't have kids and who can explore things. I can't. I have two little kids." I'll tell you another reason I didn't think I could be part of it. I was getting a lot of magazines from the States 'cos they were just that little bit more ahead in making magazines, and as far as I could see all the lesbians they represented were young, lithe, long hair blowing in the wind, standing by the water's edge, not a stretch mark on their tummy. I was only in my early thirties but I felt terribly past it and old and I thought that that wasn't an image I had of myself.

Then of course I developed an incredibly passionate crush on this woman in my consciousness raising group, in my small local group at Tufnell Park. Looking back on it, she was boyishly butch and she was an out lesbian and I fantasised like mad, I really did. I just thought maybe something would happen but I didn't know how it was going to happen. I just didn't have a clue! And nothing happened and she got together with another woman, and as far as I know she never realised how much I lusted after her.

Later, not too much, I met another woman who'd been in Holloway Prison. We were meeting up but I didn't have a clue, as usual, that anything was going to happen. We were in Camden Town in The Black Cap and I said something like, "You know, I'm finding you very attractive," and she sort of spun around because she was so pleased. Then she asked me to take her to a lesbian disco down in South London. I can't remember the name of it but it was around the Oval somewhere. Anyway, I said, "All right," like I knew all about it. I was filled with trepidation because I'd been to lots of Women's Liberation huge dances where women all danced together and took their shirts off and everything, but to go to a designated lesbian place, I hadn't done that before. She was butch, tall, a little bit heavy set, big breasts and she had that sort of intensity, that kind of stare. So I then went around with knickers absolutely soaking wet for about a month.

Then there was a Women's Liberation conference in London. My kids were about six and eight and I said to my husband that I was going to go to it and I didn't want to keep coming home at night and I was going to stay at a friend's house near the conference. I went and stayed with her and that was it. I was completely and utterly captivated and never looked back. I had been thinking all the time about what it would be like to be made love to, I was thinking about being seduced and swept away, you know? I'd practically swoon at the thought of all this, but what I didn't realise was how fabulous it was going to be to make love to a woman.

I had a wonderful, wonderful husband and really he didn't only do his fair share, he did a hell of a lot more than his fair share. Quite spontaneously. I really loved my husband, so once I knew I was a lesbian, I stayed with him for about two years. I'd still go off with girlfriends. The whole situation was impossible, horrible, for everybody. And he knew. He was terribly upset. But we're extremely close now and all of us meet up for a meal regularly.

STEPH:

I knew that I always liked a certain type of person, sort of slightly athletic, sort of either very feminine men or butch women. That was the sort I liked. And my ex-husband had come into the quite feminine men category.

JACK:

For most of my twenties and well into my thirties I had this totally bisexual attitude but which was more successful and more pleasurable with men than with women. I don't know whether I was setting out to prove something by dating women or whether it was the time that we were all growing up in. This was the late Fifties. I think in those days we felt we had a kind of responsibility to our families, to our parents.

TAZ:

In my own self I never felt a turmoil about me being gay or anything like that. My only problem was, because I had girlfriends too, I didn't know whether I wanted to get married and have a child and all that sort of stuff. Would I tell the girl there was this other side of me?

PEGGY:

I grew up completely ignorant about lesbians really. I was bringing up my family and it wasn't until I was twenty-five or six that I ever heard the word, I think. I saw a book called *Lesbians in Literature* and I thought that was interesting, so I read that and I thought, "Oh, sounds rather nice," although it was edited by a man and he was quite selective in his works, I suppose. Then I fell in love with a women when I was about thirty-four but she was very straight. So then my youngest child was still quite young so I thought I'd wait a bit 'cos I was doing all sorts of other things at the time, finally getting educated 'cos I left school at sixteen.

Then my brother grew up and realised he was gay. I'd come across gay men in books much more than women. Then when my youngest son finally went to university, I decided to do something about it, so I looked up the gay sections in *Time Out* and that was quite interesting too. By then I'd got rid of my husband. I hated being married.

I was lucky because I found the Women's History Group at the women's centre in Holborn and I used to work in the lesbian archives on Saturday.

STEPH:
Clause 28 really fascinated me because it was introducing me, I guess, telling me about gay and lesbian themes. It sort of articulated things that I couldn't have articulated before. So actually that made me very interested in gay and lesbian things and made me then search out more information and environments.

9

QUEENS' EVIDENCE:
LESBIANS AND GAY MEN AND THE POLICE

Since the change in hate-crime law in the UK in 2003, victims of verbal or physical homophobic abuse have been encouraged by the police to report it. As mentioned in the Introduction, however, the Metropolitan Police noticed that even though some people from minority communities began letting them know about various hate crimes, there was, in proportion to other minorities, a significant lack of reporting by older LGBT people in London. The Met wanted to look into why this might be. As part of that research, they commissioned me to write and produce a film based entirely on interviews with older LGBT people about their memories and views of the police over their lifetimes. The result was a film, acted by professional actors from my theatre company, Artemis, called *Queens' Evidence*, which is still being used by officers and staff at the Met for training and education. For my work on that project, I gathered many interviews on the history of the relationship between gay men and lesbians and the police and I have included several of those extracts in this chapter and the next.

When I asked older gay men about their relationship with, and their opinion of, the police, many of their stories involved 'cottaging' and/or police entrapment. Cottaging is a gay slang term for anonymous sex between men in a public lavatory, or cruising there for sexual partners with the intention of having sex elsewhere. The term has its roots in toilet blocks resembling small cottages in their appearance. Before homosexuality was decriminalised in 1967, and even after that time, there were few places where gay men could go to meet others, either for sex or conversation, and few ways to find out where those places were that did exist. Some men I interviewed gave very honest accounts about their own experiences of cottaging and others said it was something they knew about but never personally engaged in. But it became clear to me after conducting several interviews that this activity was often central to their views on the police, since this is where many of them either encountered, or closely avoided, the possibility of being criminalised because of their sexual orientation.

The charge of 'gross indecency' was brought against any man actually caught in the act of having sex with another man; but 'importuning' was also an offence, originally established under the 1898 Vagrancy Act and 1912 Criminal Law Amendment Act, and used to prosecute men seeking sexual partners in public places. This consenting, victimless behaviour was treated as a sex crime. It is no wonder that, for so many decades, many gay men have held such a dim view of the police. But during my interviews I discovered, perhaps somewhat surprisingly, that there were also men, such as Nick, who saw their attempts at avoiding police entrapment as a kind of *"cat and mouse game"*. And Peter Y says about the police: *"I didn't have any nasty experiences with them because I was too fast for them!"*

Cottaging is an activity unique to men, and not engaged in by lesbians. This fact might be to do with the differing sexual needs of men and women and how they can be met. Indeed, there has always been an argument that lesbians have an extremely strong desire to connect emotionally with their partners, which also leads to some shocking behaviour over break-ups and, on the other hand, a tendency to remain best friends with ex-girlfriends. But whatever the difference in the make-up of lesbians and gay men, the fact remains that men left their homes (and still do), often at night, to find same-sex partners. They would usually have to go to a cottage or a common to seek out those partners and by doing so would risk the possibility of arrest and prosecution. When I originally interviewed Ian for the play *Gateway to Heaven*, he gave me some of his stories and opinions around this subject. He said, *"If one's honest, there was a certain fascination about the danger."* For the play, I decided to leave out that particular quotation in case it might have been seen as slightly controversial, but I have included it in this book because a few more of the men I interviewed later expressed similar views on the subject.

When I was working on gathering interviews for the film for the Metropolitan Police, I was aware that, because of the history of gay male sex having been illegal, the script could easily become male-dominated. In an attempt to redress the balance I sought out memories from lesbians about times that they too might have come into contact with the police. I have included extracts about lesbian marches, women's rights marches, women's experiences at Pride festivals over the years, and an interview with a lesbian solicitor who was involved in dealing with some of the prosecutions resulting from women's direct actions. Another interviewee is Irene, who is a Thai woman who tells of her experience of prejudice from both police and the public on the early Pride marches. (I mention that she is originally from Thailand because her pattern of speech is slightly different from that of other contributors. But I have left her words as she told them.) Linda also recalls that, on Pride marches, *"The police were not inclusive, that's what I did experience. They saw us as the dregs of society and that's how they treated us."*

And Carol, who lived in a cross-dressing community of gay men and women in London in the early 1960s, recalls: *"You'd come out The Boltons or The Coleherne at eleven o'clock, closing time, and there'd be loads and loads of coppers just waiting to see if they could arrest people for being in drag, anything, they'd arrest you for anything at all. It was really awful. Just 'cos you were gay."*

As mentioned previously, Carol was a lesbian who dressed in men's clothes. She was then seen by the police, and possibly society as well, as someone who was so different from the accepted mainstream as to be a potential criminal. As she then explains in this chapter, the knock-on effect was that, dressed as a man, she couldn't find work, so in order to live and to eat she turned to petty crime. Now, decades later, we might say about her, "Well, that bit certainly wasn't necessary. We do feel sorry for her not being accepted by society but people should keep on the right side of the law, whatever their circumstances." But for some lesbians and gay men who could not work, had no money to feed themselves, were thrown out of accommodation when people found out they were in drag and had to sleep on park benches, criminality was the life they were drawn into.

The Gay London Police Monitoring Group (GALOP) was created in 1982 to expose the systematic harassment of the gay and lesbian communities by the police and to educate people about their rights. But some of the contributors note that by the mid 1990s the police had begun the process of addressing their negative attitudes towards LGBT people. This was particularly perceived on Pride marches where, as Jeffrey comments, *"You didn't get the feeling then that the police were hostile to us, holding us in, they were becoming increasingly part of it, a normal part of their duties, policing a public event."* And on 26 July 2003 it became clear that the tide had truly turned, when lesbian and gay police officers themselves marched for the first time in full uniform on the London Gay Pride March.

CS

~

Interviews

Cottaging

JIMMY:

I was born on 23 January 1920. There was all the early days of gays where we were persecuted of course in lots of ways. I got into trouble a couple of times. I got caught what they called 'importuning' in Earls Court – this was just after the war actually and it was an *agent provocateur*.

We met in the cemetery, 'cos it was two or three doors down from The Coleherne, and the cemetery was well known as a place to pick up. It was in the 'cottages', they called it. I went in the toilet and he signalled to go outside, and we went outside and I was sat on the seat talking, and he was reading a book and I was asking what book it was and so on. I even gave him some sweets and then we went into another toilet, which I hadn't seen before, and it was a small one, with just one stall and one lock-up toilet, and somebody was in there and we couldn't get them out. So then I came out and went out to enter Fulham Road and he walked behind me and he said, "I'm arresting you for importuning." So I had to go to court. But we hadn't had sex of any kind. The ruling was that if you were in a loo and you came out with somebody, signalled them to come out, rather than play around with them there, it was called importuning. Importuning for immoral purposes.

I had another offence a few years afterwards. It was about 1948, after I came out of the army. I'd been six and a half years in the army. I was living at Shepherds Bush at the time and Putney towpath used to be a place where you could cruise. I went along there by Hammersmith Bridge and walked right the way along and a cyclist came along and he said, "Don't stay down there, let's go right up there," and we went up to Barnes. There was a depository with big grounds and we went over there and again attempted to have sex but nothing happened, we couldn't. It turned out that he was married with four children and I asked the police not to arrest him, but they swore that we were having sex, and in actual fact we weren't.

I was very scared in those days and we just wanted to get the case over and be as anonymous as possible – and of course I thought my landlady could find out, but fortunately it didn't come in the papers. So anyway, the magistrate said, "Oh, this is your second offence, I'm going to send you to Wandsworth Prison for a week for a psychiatrist's report." You've got to remember it was against the law and so on and I was put in next to, believe it or not, a transsexual – this is true – and he got ribbed because of the make-up and so on, and one of the warders was having sex with him. All the inmates in the different cells, they all knew that this was going on.

We used to get paraded once a day round there and they'd

say, "What are you in for?" and I'd say, "Embezzlement." 'Cos I couldn't think of anything else and I didn't want to tell them I was gay. Anyway, I saw the psychiatrist and I told him that I've always been gay. I said to him, "Well there's nothing you can do about it." To cut a long story short, I went back to court and I was fined – I think it was a hundred and something pounds, anyway it was a lot of money in those days – and discharged.

You'd hear stories, well you'd read them, because a lot of people got into the newspapers. That was what worried me, because if you had any trouble at all, the press, especially the local newspapers, they'd have a field day with it all, have your name and address printed, you know? Of course it was a worry and you knew if the police got you, they would swear your life away, I can tell you, and you couldn't challenge them, you were so afraid that if you challenged them something else would happen. In other words, the police, they really told lies, no doubt about it. I mean it was an easy cop in those days, they could arrest anyone who was gay. Usually it was in the toilets but there were the open commons and all that. I only had the two experiences with the police and they were very nice. They'd give you a cigarette, I used to smoke in those days and all that. They said, "If you own up to it you'll get off lightly but if you don't it'll go to another court." So it was sort of a little bit of blackmail really to gay people.

I think a lot of it was out of loneliness really. Like most gay people there were times when it was frustrating and you used to go out hunting for sex like everybody else. I was promiscuous, of course I was, but not overly so, but it all had to be secret. In those days you were terrified of being caught, like so many people. As I've said before, I think it was a lot of people lived on their own, it was desperation really, loneliness, yes, going back to a flat on your own. You're only human after all.

BOB H:

I do know people who went into a loo, were chatted up by a dolly-looking person who turned out to be a police officer, came out and were then charged, which was outrageous. There were certainly regular raids on cruising areas by police who, in my view, saw it as a form of Saturday night sport, possibly after they'd had a couple of drinks. That happened in Hampstead, Mitcham Common, places like that. They took great pleasure in knowing if there was a cruising area, say Hampstead Heath, screaming along there in a van with all the lights on – I think they'd had a couple of pints before they went as well – to watch everyone scamper, and if someone didn't move fast enough they'd probably arrest them. They'd think they were doing society a service. I think that my attitude that the Metropolitan Police were a bloody disgraceful bunch of uniformed thugs who were racist, homophobic and probably sexist, up until ten years ago was probably quite right.

There was one guy I knew of who went into a cottage somewhere, can't remember where, was then beaten up by thugs, smashed nose, whatever, but then rather than report it as a serious assault, he pretended he'd banged his head on the steering wheel 'cos he wasn't wearing his seatbelt, rather than report it, because he didn't trust the police to even bother to take it seriously. That's very common, I think that's universal, because you'd probably get, "Well, if you behave like that, you deserve it, don't you? What do you expect?"

BOB L:

Before the '67 act everything was illegal and even after that if you were caught, which fortunately I wasn't, but if you were – and I know people who have been – you'd go before a magistrate's court and they would automatically assume that the police were right. And if they had an *agent provocateur* it was an easy arrest.

I've heard from police who I work with and from friends and that's what they did. They would have one policeman sort of showing a flash of something and then as soon as you approached – they obviously weren't in uniform – as you approached, another policeman in uniform would come up and say, "Right you, that's it." By the time they were in the court the police tended to embroider what had happened and then the magistrate generally would accept every word. If you said anything in your defence it went against you, so that's why people used to appeal to go to the next stage, the Assizes or the Crown Court as it then became, because there was more chance to get a professional judge.

I used to appoint the JPs and whilst we tried to appoint those who reflected the area, most of them, because they'd got the time, tended to be middle class, people who would accept anything the police said. "How can the police possibly lie?" And, "These ghastly people, dreadful, immoral people, they must obviously be guilty." So that was the attitude. Most people didn't fight, they would just plead guilty, get the minimum fine. It was probably a fine and a caution and hopefully that was it and it wouldn't be in the paper – because if it was, that was their lives ruined. I had been in cottages when they'd been raided but fortunately I got out. Somebody would say "Police!" when they were a few yards away and if you were careful, well if you were lucky, you could just walk out. They can't really do much if you've gone out.

Personally, I don't think I was against the police. I used to be annoyed in the Sixties to some extent, when everyone was calling them pigs and that, but again it wasn't their fault that they were told to disperse CND people or anything like that. I think I somehow, I don't know if I'm using retrospect, I could separate the people from the job. They had a job to do and they did it. I'm not saying I would have been highly delighted if I had been caught cottaging, and with that policeman or group of policemen I probably would have hated them, but I wasn't caught, so that was the thing.

EMMANUEL:

By the late Sixties cottaging was a very well-established network within London. There were cottages on practically every corner and the whole of the Circle Line and on many of the stations there was a cottage. So there was one on Baker Street, there was one on Great Portland Street, there was one on Kings Cross and there was one on Farringdon. On some of them they were on the platforms and on some of them you had to leave the platform to go to it. They were just men's toilets. There was one on Oxford Circus as well. So you could stay on the train and go to all these different cottages, and I remember on one occasion I met this man and we had sex in the cottage, and it was usually just standing up at the urinal, and he said, "OK then, love, see you in chapel." To him they were a chapel and I thought how extraordinary, and it was his euphemism! I thought it was all terribly satisfactory because I had all this sexual excitement and no responsibility. I mean, it was all masturbatory sex, there wasn't anything other than that. I was terrified of getting into trouble with the police. They did entrap people.

The first time I went to Hampstead Heath I was taken by a friend and I remember walking on the heath and thinking, "Christ, this is terrifying," and rushing off thinking, "This is not for me." But it was a free-for-all and it offered all these opportunities, so I did go there and have good times, but basically I realised that I'm not that interested in anonymous sex and that I find that I'm either too inhibited or don't relate to people enough. So that although for some years it had its attraction and it fulfilled a need, it wasn't in itself that interesting for me.

ROGER:

When I was seventeen to eighteen, I worked in a solicitor's office in London in Bedford Square and I was not just naive, I was thick! This particular evening I was given the post, because I was the junior. I was going to night school, and they said, "Will you take this to the post as you go?" So I put them in the letterbox and went round the corner to go through the back door or gate in the wall of the school. There was also a public toilet there. Lots of public toilets in London at that time. So I thought I'd go into the loo before I go into the school. So I went into the toilet and it was packed. I didn't take any notice, went all the way down to the end, pee'd and came out. As I was coming out all these heads watched me, well they watched me coming in, watched me going out. I thought, "Don't know what they're all staring at me for." I came out and I was aware that somebody had followed me out. So I went into the playground, aware that somebody was following me, went into the school, and the classroom that we used was the one by the door, so the windows looked out on the playground on the ground floor. Well, I could see this man standing outside making faces at me. So when I got home I told my mother and we all discussed it and she said, "You'd better go and tell the police." Because none of us could work out what this was about, this strange man following me.

This was the 1950s. My mother wouldn't have known anything, she was as frigid as an old boot. How she managed to produce three children I've no idea. But anyway, I told the policemen and they sat there and, bless them, they didn't laugh. "I expect they were gambling, Sir. We'll look into it." And that's how naive I was!

IAN:
It's so weird, cottaging. If you're looking for a male partner, if you're phallic fascinated, what better opportunity to find if somebody's interested than by standing in a public toilet and seeing if they're aroused and you're aroused? It's so easy that way, if you just want a quick bit of whatever. It's strange, but if one's looking for casual sex, it was a very easy shortcut. On the other hand, the fact that the police used that and used it to entrap people made it very dangerous, but then again, you know, if one's honest, there was a certain fascination about the danger. I mean, when you were illegal there was a certain frisson of excitement about that, the idea of meeting somebody.

BOB C:

I was arrested in a cottage in 1977 and decided to plead not guilty on a gross indecency charge. I was coming back from a club at Manor House and I was going back to where I lived, which was near Finsbury Park, and I went into this cottage just to see what was going on, really. And this man then followed me in and within about a minute the police sort of swooped in on the place, so it was obviously a place where they knew they could make lots of arrests. I pleaded not guilty, partly from outrage because I wasn't doing what they said I was doing. The evidence was really quite lurid and I suppose we were kind of looking at each other, me and this guy, but we were not doing what they said.

But the other reason I made that decision was, I suppose, because I had been through GLF politics, I thought, "No, I'm not just going to plead guilty quietly." There was no guarantee that if I had pleaded guilty quietly there would have been no repercussions, because as a teacher I didn't know what would have happened, but it was the politics of it. After a year the case was thrown out. There was a jury but the judge instructed the jury to acquit me because of the paucity of the police evidence.

The other man I was arrested with had a much worse time than me because he was a catering worker, so he worked in the seaside resorts in the summer and came up to London in the winter to get work – and this was in October when it happened. He had just come to London and hadn't even got himself a proper place to stay, but of course when he got arrested without a proper address they kept him in Brixton Prison for a week.

NICK:

Certainly you had the occasional person who used to say, "Just watch out. The police do come up here and you do get the occasional *agent provocateur*." I was aware of the term but you could always tell a policeman who was trying to trap you. There's a certain woodenness to someone who's trying to cruise who's never cruised before. They're very sort of stiff and generally speaking they were sort of eyes everywhere, just walking in and would make the extra special sort of wish to make eye contact. Most cruising is done in such a way that it's a fleeting glance, just enough to communicate. It's not a long cow-eyed stare, but you'd get the police who were doing this and you're just thinking, "Sorry, this is just sort of ridiculous!"

The only other way you could get caught was if they were raiding you, and that was how I was caught. The police did a raid at the toilets at Cherry Orchard Road in Croydon. It was actually quite frightening because, in essence, gay guys in a cottage, there's a certain camaraderie. OK, you're having sex with the person, but there's something very strange and intoxicating about the alluring... the excitement about anonymous sex in a darkened environment, where you have no idea who you're with. So you've got the fear aspect of the potential excitement that you might get caught and you don't know who you're going to be caught with and the whole thing was almost like a cat and mouse game. The fear aspect creates a sort of sense of how quickly can you do what you need to get done before you then suddenly either have to make a move, or prove ignorance or innocence?

I was caught fair and square. They raided with torches – and with torches, people do freeze immediately. It literally was the scared rabbit mentality. The guy I was with breathed a hefty sigh of relief when I said I was twenty-one, 'cos at that time the age of consent was twenty-one. But I do remember trying to sneak out and this policeman grabbed my arm and hurled me back against the wall and I remember him saying, "I've got you, you little poofter bastard. There's no way you're fucking getting away from anything I'm going to throw at you." I was held there and he said, "Don't even move or I'm going to cuff you and you are going to pay."

It was my first and only time I was locked in a cell, at Norbury Police Station, but I do remember being treated with a great deal of courtesy; asked for my fingerprints, had the pictures taken and they said, "Yes, we've arrested you but there's nothing you need to worry about. OK, you got caught, but just don't get caught again." And I was thinking, "Well, this is from one extreme, where someone is going to end my living days, to almost treating it like a joke." It was a very confusing experience at the time – and certainly for a twenty-one-year-old, who was only just legal at that point.

We then had to go to court and I pleaded guilty because I thought that's what I had to do. There was a duty solicitor who said, "Oh well, you've been caught cottaging, just plead guilty." So it wasn't until afterwards when I talked to people about it and they said, "You should never have done that, you should have pleaded not guilty." I said, "Well, why?" They said the reason for it was that your life could be affected because you're on the sex offenders register and you'll not be able to do certain things in your life.

Attitudes towards and from the Police

STANLEY:
In those days there was a policeman who was head of the vice squad. Dick. There used to be a vice squad in Soho. I became very friendly with him because he used to come to The Rockingham and have a drink and so on, and one night I remember going home with him, and it was about half past one in the morning, and I said, "Goodnight Dick," and he said, "Aren't you going to ask me up?" So I said, "Do come in if you like." So he came up into the drawing room and he said, "It's a bit chilly in here, why don't we go in your bedroom?" Imagine my astonishment! This was the chief of the vice squad in my bedroom – and he had everything off in two minutes flat!

PETER Y:
Well, I'd heard about incidents of entrapment but it didn't affect me directly. I mean, there was one case where I met someone who, in the Fifties I think, in one of the provincial towns, had been questioned, he was only young at the time. He'd been

questioned because he'd been named by some other people in a so-called ring. Other people when asked and questioned had included his name, you see? So he'd then been questioned, he was a young lad. He wasn't prosecuted or didn't go to prison or anything, but it really affected his health. He went temporarily bald because he'd gone through all this hassle.

One knew that you had to steer clear of the police and you did, it was as simple as that. I didn't have any nasty experiences with them because I was too fast for them! Well, put it this way, you'd go to these places and you'd think, "It might happen or it might not." I never went to a cottage thinking that I was going to have sex with someone come what may, but if I was on my way to somewhere or if I had spare time, I'd go to a cottage and maybe there would be a gorgeous man there and something might happen. Nine times out of ten it wouldn't, so it was just an off-chance sort of thing – and there again, you'd be discreet. If you went into a cottage and saw a lot of people there, you'd nip in and nip out. You wouldn't sort of blatantly do things in front of other people, but if you happened to go in there and it was eleven-thirty at night and there was one other person there or two other people there or so on... The places I'm thinking of were ones which had no reputation whatsoever for being raided. The police weren't raiding all these places all the time.

In London at railway stations and on various streets there'd be cottages, and you'd pop in there and have a little look around. You weren't all: "Oh you've got to beware, there's a policeman on every corner!" Well, there was always a chance they might be there but they weren't there all the time. What I'm saying is that I don't think in the Sixties and the Seventies we lived in constant fear of the police.

CAROL:
Gay men could be arrested if they wore female drag, if they didn't have male underpants on – if they had female underpants on, they could be arrested. If they had drag, women's clothes and they wore men's underpants, they couldn't be arrested,

and the same with us. Although it wasn't against the law for women to dress in drag, you could get a lot of harassment and a few of the girls were searched, taken into police stations and stuff, and if they had male underwear on, they'd cause a lot of problems. It was awful, the pressure and the harassment.

Once, we'd come out The Boltons, I'd had a little drink, everyone drank, it's the gay scene isn't it? Drink, drink, drink. So we'd come out The Boltons and we walked down Earls Court Road. Now, the only loo open was the men's, so me and Paddy, she was in drag as well, go into the male toilet. We'd gone straight into the cubicle of course, but some straight guys saw us going in, called the cops and they arrested us, took us in a bloody white Maria, took us in. Everyone was in uproar, screaming and shouting because Earls Court was full of mostly queens. They locked us up for the night, we had nothing, we just had what we had on to wear. So even if we'd wanted to change to go into court we couldn't. So we go into court the next morning and the judge was there and the whole gay population has turned up. It was just amazing! It was like something out of a film set. It had got round that everyone had been arrested and everyone took days off work and the court was full of queens and a few gay women. So the judge said to Paddy (her name was Pat really, her drag name was Paddy, mine was Caz, see?), he said, "Miss Paddy Dufton, I see you come from Belfast."

So she said, "Yes, your honour."

He said, "Why didn't you go home to go to the toilet?"

And I think she said something like, "Well, Belfast is a long way to go for a pee."

And the court was in uproar. It was fantastic and I think they fined us a pound each. A pound was a lot of money in them days. I said to him, "There was no women's toilets open, it was the only toilet available, and we had to go in there."

Generally speaking the police were really bad in them days against gays. You'd be in The Casino, all the lights would come on, all the police would come down, about twenty, thirty coppers, might have a hundred people in there. The police would come in, they'd ask you your age, your name, where you lived – and if you didn't have an address to give them, they'd arrest you on the spot, or if you didn't have ten bob. It was a vagrancy law, if you didn't have a certain amount of money on you, you could be arrested and they'd check you out, because a lot of the kids were on the run. They'd come down in this great big white police van and they'd park it in Wardour Street, block the mews where The Casino was, and they'd just take loads and loads of people off and that was really frightening.

I was never taken off because I always had money on me and I always gave them the right answers, but a lot of people were, and they were checked out and sent back home and they'd come from terrible homes where they were anti-gay. So you'd see people one night and you wouldn't see them again, they'd be gone, they'd be arrested. That happened quite a lot. And you'd come out The Boltons or The Coleherne at eleven o'clock, closing time, and there'd be loads and loads of coppers just waiting to see if they could arrest people for being in drag, anything, they'd arrest you for anything at all. It was really awful. Just 'cos you were gay.

I was in prison for a week. What happened was that living in Earls Court in drag it was very difficult to find work and so quite a lot of the gays would go nicking and they'd have mail rounds. What mail rounds were (a lot of people did it), you'd have a certain area where you went round Kensington, Chelsea, where there was a lot of money and as the postman went in the house to put all the mail in ('cos all the doors were open in those days) you'd go in and get all the mail and there'd often be giros and money and all sorts of stuff.

We didn't only do that; if I wanted some new shirts or something you'd go around the big houses and at the back their laundry would come once a week, full up with all their laundry, and I would just take out what I wanted, shirts and all sorts, and if there was anything really good, we'd take the whole fucking basket and take it back to the flat. All the queens would have something and all the girls would have something and we'd have all our clothes like that. Then we'd get the bread round. The baker would drop all the bread round in the shop and we'd take the whole tray and everyone would have bread for a week!

Why we had to do this was because we couldn't get work. All the men were in drag and trannies, sex changes, and some of the girls were too. So work was virtually impossible. Signing on was a waste of time, you didn't get very much. So the only way to make a living was crime and everyone did something. A lot of the gay women were prostitutes. They did clip joints, stuff like that. Well, I couldn't get into that. My only way round it was getting what I could other ways. So I became a cat burglar. Yeah, it was great! Met this guy who'd done it all his life, a gay guy, and I was very interested and he was telling me all about it and I said, "I'd love to come with you," and he said, "All right then." I was young and thin and energetic. So we used to climb up buildings in Earls Court, get a rope up, you'd climb, you'd get in windows, you'd nick what you could and you'd go out the back door or the front door. One house we went into (I stopped it after that), I mean a really rich house, plenty of money, ornaments, and we went in and they were all in the lounge sitting and watching bloody telly and he said to me, "Come on, walk straight through and out the front door." I nearly died, but I didn't go nicking again after that.

I shared a basement flat in Pembroke Gardens, Earls Court, with three gay guys and three gay women and they were all into doing all sorts of things. The queens were OK, they could work in the theatre. Feminine girls were OK, they could get whatever jobs and Paddy, like me, was in drag, and we'd do our own thing. We came back to the flat one day and there were about fifty coppers in there and I said, "What's going on?" And they said, "We've arrested Miss Paddy Dufton. We have found bank books." I used to do forging and all sorts; bank books, Giros, all sorts of stuff. "Do you have anything to do with it?" Well, I was very naive and I stuck by my friends and I said, "Yes, yes I do." But I didn't, it was nothing to do with me. Because whatever I did, I used to rip the stuff up and I'd put it down the loo. In fact I had a load of stuff on me as I walked in. So I walked into the loo and ripped it all up and as I'm ripping it all up and trying to put it down the bloody loo, pulling the chain about three or four times trying to get rid of it, there's two coppers coming up the back window behind me. I just got rid of it in time.

But I said I'd done it as well 'cos I wanted to stick by her. I just thought we were friends, a false sense of loyalty really, you know, when you're young? Well, they had no proof that I'd done anything to be honest, but we got taken away in this police van to Holloway Prison and we were there for a week. In those days you had to wear pink flowery dresses and there was me in this big butch role, and all of a sudden all these butches were in these bloody women's dresses. From drag to dresses! You know? We worked in the sack factory. I wrote to my parents and told them. They didn't come to visit me. Didn't matter. Then by the end of the week we'd earned, I don't know, enough to buy half an ounce of tobacco. But while I was there, this woman who was a lifer took a fancy to me. I was on D Wing and she asked me would I help her with the milk round? So that meant getting up at five o'clock, but it was better than being in your cell. So I went out with her and she'd given me some tobacco for helping out with the milk round. It was nearly all gay women that were in there. Unbelievable. Then we had to go to court and I was given a conditional discharge which lasted, I think, ten years. If you didn't do anything during that time then you were let off and it was wiped out, so they say. But I didn't actually get charged.

But it was fun. It was one of my ambitions. I know it sounds stupid but when I was young I always fancied going to Holloway Prison! I think that's probably one of the reasons I said yes, I was involved. It was a camp place to be, and there were all sorts of women who'd killed their girlfriends, some who were really weird and tough women in there. You had to toughen up while you were in there. There were prostitutes that we knew from the West End and some of the girls had lovely cells with all sorts of pictures and flowers, they'd saved up their money and made it like a little home if you like.

But yes, it was quite an experience, and when we came out our landlady had thrown us out and we had nowhere to live and we were sent to a Salvation Army hospital and had to say prayers and all that. We stayed one night and then we left there. I don't know where my girlfriend went. We split up for a while and I slept in Hyde Park for about two weeks on a bench. I was never afraid because lots of people did it in those days. It was summer anyway. So we just slept in the park and worked away and saved up money to get another place. But you were often evicted and thrown out and you had to survive whichever way you could really. No support from family or anything like that. So you had to make your own way through.

BOB H:

My attitude to the police was already soured because somewhere around the mid Seventies, when I was about twenty-seven, I had a boyfriend who was nineteen or twenty who turned out to be a violent domestic abuser. I didn't realise it was domestic abuse at the time, I do now because we've got a definition of it. He was totally jealous, a total lunatic, he'd drink a bottle of Martini and fly off the handle, wreck the house, attacked me loads of times. I got dislocated fingers, cuts, bruises, absolutely horrendous. I was working in a school where this lunatic is threatening to come down. In fact, one day he did walk in and I was in charge of a Year Eight assembly and he turned up drunk from the night before, at ten o'clock in the morning, and bashed through the back, with no bloody shoes on!

I was getting burgled, threatened, blackmailed, assaulted and the people who should have been able to help or protect me were the police, but this lunatic, unbeknown to me, had already done this to somebody else and so this other guy was in jail. I think when he did it he was only sixteen or seventeen and the guy was older and he'd mouthed off this very plausible weepy type thing that *he'd* been abused. The age of consent was twenty-one and he was under twenty-one so he was using that: "You can't go to the police 'cos if you do I'm going to tell them that." So the very people who should have protected me from all that outrageous stuff I didn't dare go to, because I did not trust them not to turn it around and go: "Well, you've had sex with him, that's an offence, you're in jail."

When he turned twenty-one I was free of it. But the reason I was subjected to that was that I could not trust the police. If I went to them they could just say, "Right, we're doing you and that's illegal." Now, whether they would have done or whether they wouldn't have I don't know, but the fact is I couldn't trust them enough to do it. So I blame them fairly and squarely for me having to put up with that and being denied the sort of protection I should have had in law.

Pride Marches and Feminist Demonstrations

BOB H:
I went along to the very first gay march and I sort of edged up and had a little look. I suppose it was a mixture of curiosity and a kind of awakening that you need to stand up for things and you knew other people were doing it, something like that. At the early Pride marches there was the feeling that we were a small unruly sort of ramshackly group of marchers and there was a disapproving police presence. "What's all this about?" Yeah. Well, certainly not approval. We might as well have been the BNP from the approval we got from the police. Their attitude was sour. Sour and disapproving. "What's this we've got to deal with now?"

IRENE:
In the Eighties, I was one of the first bunch of people that organised the Gay Pride at the Embankment. It was only half a dozen of us together, we used to set up our little stall. Everything was voluntary and then we'd go back to Parliament Square to our march and march to County Hall, it used to be, before they abolished it.

In those days I think the police were not very keen to protect us because we had quite a lot of trouble to get permission for the police to protect the march to come to County Hall. They were not very willing to do that. They just said that it's "a waste of tax-payers' money" and they said: "We don't want any trouble-makers. This sort of demonstration is not really welcome." We tried to put it that, "This is not a demonstration, this is just a peaceful march to make people aware that we're here to stay," and a few of them were willing to do it but we had a lot of difficulty to help them to police, stop the traffic and things like that. They were just there, they didn't make any effort and it was such a short march anyway, the only thing we wanted them to do is just stop the traffic while we were crossing the main road. Once we got into County Hall they just went back to their headquarters until about three or four years later because the gay march became bigger and bigger and they had to take notice. Then we formed a committee but it wasn't very welcome, to be quite honest with you, up until... it must have been about eight years later, they realised that this is not just a passing-through thing.

You still got quite a lot of abuse language from the public and when you get to report it to the police, when you can find some police around, they more or less say, "There's nothing we can do about it." I remember a couple of incidents. One was when we marched to Kennington Park. When we finished the march we went to the park for a party. People on the roadside sell drinks and things like that from the house and I never forget this woman said to her son, his name was Darren, "Darren, stay away from those people. They got disease, they might jump out and get to you." I was so angry, I turned round and said, "Is it all right for you to take our money? You're selling stuff." They said, "Well, basically, we just don't want to know your kind." Then I saw a policeman and I told him and he said, "There's nothing we can do about it. It's not violent, it's just verbal abuse, it's not even abuse."

Another incident was when people used to say, "Kill those bloody queers!" on the march, "They shouldn't be allowed to live." That made me feel anger. I would have given them an answer back, but I can't turn round and start a riot because that is not fair on everybody. We wanted a peaceful march and to make an incident, it doesn't look good. So I had to say, "Why do you behave like this? What have any of us done to harm you?" You try to reason with them but it does no good because they don't want to listen.

GRIFF:
Over the years I've been very much involved in organising Pride marches. There's a very good photograph from the early Seventies, coming up Regent Street passing Austin Reed, you can see the CHE banners, but you can't see the people for the police who are all around them. I think it's been done as a poster. It was a Gay Pride one but there would be mostly CHE groups and GLF on the march, but there were just four sides of police in helmets. You can just see the CHE banner but you can't see the people because of the policemen with their helmets on and the police's answer was: "We're there to protect you from the others watching."

VAL:
I was going around with a group of younger lesbians trying to set up a lesbian centre in Camden, something I couldn't imagine happening actually, but we did get it up and running in the end, after much hard work, you know? Anyway, they were Greenham women and more aware of the law and police tactics than me. I was very naive and new to it all. When we went to Pride we used to take this card called, 'Lesbians, your rights on arrest'. It was given out by Lespop (Lesbians and Policing Project). I remember being really worried that I wouldn't have time to read it if I was arrested. I was very careful to keep my head down and not do anything wrong. All the same, I look back at that time with great affection. It was a time of great change for me.

The police were pretty heavy-handed, you know? As if they were expecting trouble. This would have been in the late

Eighties. They used to keep horses round the back ready for charging and sometimes that happened. There was one Pride down in Kennington one year and that was very scary because it was a small space for it to be held and I think there was an actual charge by the police with horses. I mean, we were luckily not too close. But to see it, to know that we weren't doing any harm and they were up in arms, as it were! Any silly little incident seemed to set them off, you know? They were ready for trouble. I mean, they'd police the march of course but there was always this other contingent ready for trouble.

LINDA:

I do remember Pride marches where you would anticipate that the police would attack us at the end or at least allow circumstances to occur in which police horses would be turned on our community rather than on those who might be attacking us, whether that was the BNP or whoever. On one march I remember the violence of the police and I can remember a particularly beautiful horse rearing up towards us. It was very clear that the police were hostile to us, didn't see us as equal citizens and worthy of protection, and if they ever attacked us they would be largely indifferent to our safety. I remember several occasions on which they were just disgusting. I can't put it more strongly than that. They were just truncheons and police horses into our community and I really didn't expect it.

My parents had taught me to be respectful of the police. You respect elders and so on and that's how you were brought up. But I was a citizen, I was born in this country. I had rights so I was very clear about what I thought they ought to be doing; and what I thought they ought to be doing and what they were doing was quite different.

It would be fair to say that I did not have very positive experiences of policing as a lesbian. As a black person my experience was even worse. The police were not inclusive, that's what I did experience. They saw us as the dregs of society and that's how they treated us. But I'm delighted to say that the police have significantly changed, including more and more police officers who are lesbian and gay, and many police officers who are not lesbian and gay and are really good police officers, who are sensitive and helpful. But it's not accidental, lots of work has been done to make it happen.

JEFFREY:

In the Fifties and Sixties, of course, the police were a threat then, because they could bang on your door and arrest you for having sex with your partner. And that did happen on many, many occasions, and I've heard stories of people who felt really threatened when a policeman walked down the street. Were they going to call on my door? Or if a policeman knocked on your door for whatever reason, you were dreading that they would notice that there was a double bed and two men were living in a bedsitter or that there might be a physique magazine sitting on the shelf or whatever, and there was a real fear of one of these chain arrests. The police might arrest someone cottaging, say, look at their address book and then have a long list of addresses that they'd follow up.

I think in the early Seventies, Gay Liberation saw itself as a left-wing movement, part of the wider radical revolutionary movement and yes, the police were part of the enemy. Part of the rhetoric came from the United States where police were called 'pigs' and so on, and you'd find radicals using the same sort of language. One of the early discos of Gay Liberation in 1971 was raided by the police ostensibly looking for drugs and we all had to empty our pockets. My memory is fading, but it felt like there were a lot of police, ten or twelve, and of course this was in the days before drugs were associated with clubbing so I don't think any drugs were found. They may have been discreetly thrown on the floor, but it wasn't a druggy atmosphere. It was a heady atmosphere because we were all together. Nothing followed from that. I don't think there were any arrests or anything, but there were other incidents in those early Gay Liberation events when the police were heavy, like the early Gay Liberation marches. The police walked alongside you, and you weren't sure whether the protection was also a constraint, trapping you in. They'd come up to you of course and say, "You're wandering a bit too much from the centre, you can't go over there." So in the early Seventies the police held people in and today the police are part of the parades and that's such a radical transformation, you just have to pinch yourself sometimes to think about it!

My generation assumed that the police would be hostile and there was no expectation at that stage that the police would be on our side. In the 1980s the impact of AIDS had a major impact on social attitudes and by the mid 1980s of course, the chief constable of Greater Manchester Police, in the context of AIDS, talked about "gays swilling around in a cesspool of their own making". So that was very much the attitude that we experienced from seeing a policeman, and with the Metropolitan Police, I don't remember so much that sort of rhetoric, but it certainly didn't seem a friendly police force, as late as the Eighties. So the attitudes only fundamentally began to change in the early Nineties.

The huge Pride events on Clapham Common and in Jubilee Gardens in the Nineties were really festivals and the police would often walk around quite relaxed. You didn't get the feeling then that the police were hostile to us, holding us in, they were becoming increasingly part of it, a normal part of their duties, policing a public event. I think by the early Nineties we'd become almost a respectable part of the wider social scene. There was a recognition that Britain was becoming much more diverse, ethnically, racially, socially and culturally and we were part of that increased diversity and therefore it was becoming increasingly the police's duty to work with us, not against us.

Of course, lots of people had worked hard at that: GALOP and so on, Stonewall, and even the more confrontational politics of Outrage! was beginning to take for granted that the police would protect them rather than be against them. So there was a shift taking place, but I think there was also a shift going on in the Metropolitan Police leadership which was probably becoming a bit more aware of the community and diversity. I can't remember any major statements but I know that some time in the Nineties the police said that they wouldn't be harassing gay men on Hampstead Heath and they started giving out more fatherly advice rather than strict policing. "You shouldn't be doing this, why are you doing this?" That sort of thing, rather than, "This is illegal and we're going to get you for it." I think there was a change of tone taking place in the Nineties.

NIC:
In the late Seventies, I was on a feminist march and it was a bit heated. There were a couple of women who rushed into some porn shops, inside, throwing some books around the floor and the police sort of chased us down an alleyway with truncheons and they just hit women on the head. It was really terrifying and this woman, I didn't know her, her head was split open, you know? Fracture, red skull, bleeding and everything and she was collapsed on the floor crying and blood pouring out of her head, and it was so fast and it was just a woman-hating thing really. I went to the hospital with her, I thought I had to, the Middlesex. She had to have stitches and then she had some sort of disability forever after that 'cos it can do something really harmful if you break your skull in a certain place.

There was a court case afterwards and the solicitor, lawyer who acted for us, I can't remember what her name was but we called her 'Legal Eagle', but she was a very good feminist lawyer and they, the police, were the ones that got reprimanded in the end because of the way they had handled it. In court the policeman had a male chauvinist pig tie on and the lawyer said, "Are you asking us to believe that this is an objective stance, that you're objective about this? Look at what you've got on."

And that threw the whole thing. It crumbled after that because he looked such an idiot. I think it was an anti-woman thing, a mixture of anti-lesbian and anti-woman. "These women, they're shouting and screaming." We were whistling and shouting Reclaim the Night stuff, that was all, and singing.

No, I think it was mostly an anti-woman thing, but the ferocity of it, you know? Punching and hitting women with truncheons, it was outrageous and ridiculous, because we were running away from them, what could we do?

GILL:

My experience as a lawyer of dealing with the police in the Seventies for women was that they had zero understanding, for example, of domestic violence. You got women ringing up and they'd tell you, "Oh, the police have said I've got to apply for an injunction." But actually, why aren't they going to prosecute? Of course, they wouldn't say. I couldn't put a date on it, but I think it was from the mid Nineties that things started to change, maybe a bit earlier than that, but there was definitely a change. I don't know what the statistics are now for the applications for injunctions but I suspect they must be minuscule compared to what we used to have to do in the Seventies – because the police wouldn't arrest men, charge them with anything, however serious.

I think women weren't taken seriously. I think they weren't taken seriously in the context of being beaten up by their husbands and I'm not so sure, but they were probably looked upon as a bit of an irritant when they did things like criminal damage. I think it was misogyny actually, that was really what it came down to. I suppose that when you think politically, you were looking at an era of a different sort of direct action, so the police got fed up policing demonstrations and things like that. So I think women coming along and throwing paint bombs was just like: Oh, something else for them to deal with!

We probably thought all policemen were terrible and they thought all demonstrators were terrible, but it was that sort of approach. You would be surprised to find a police officer who wasn't going to fit into your notion of a stereotype and indeed I'm afraid they did, most of them did fulfil the stereotypes with their attitudes towards women and particularly crimes against women.

I think most women's experience, or many women's

experience, of dealing with the police is... well, when do women come into contact with the police in their lives? It would usually be around violence against them, rather than anything else. So if you think about women's experience in the home, the police were very unenlightened about how they treated domestic violence – and women knew that.

Then the reaction was almost the same being outdoors – different, but in a way it was, "You've got to stay at home." I think there's a link there somewhere but I'm not sure what the link was, because to say the police didn't take rape and murder seriously was probably not quite true, because it's a terribly serious crime. But you know all that stuff about "You must have been asking for it" and "What were you wearing?" – which is what we still have today, this suggestion that somehow the victim has got to have caused this in some way – and maybe that's what I'm trying to say. I think that's probably the image women had of the police: if you're at home and you're assaulted they didn't want to get involved and if you're on the streets, "Well, what did you do to cause it?"

10

RANK OUTSIDERS:
LIFE IN THE ARMED SERVICES AND THE POLICE

In the national tour of my theatre company's play, *Gateway to Heaven*, I was extremely fortunate to have had the honour of playing the part of Vito, a woman who was dismissed from the navy for being a lesbian. Recording the interview with Vito, incorporating her feedback in the script, and performing this scene night after night on tour, gave me quite an insight into how she might have felt at the time that these terrible events happened to her, as they have happened to many other lesbians and gay men in this country. For me, the whole experience was a deeply moving one – to try to get under her skin and re-enact her story truthfully. For Vito, I think it was also a moving experience to see one of the most significant, and indeed horrendous, periods of her life being portrayed theatrically and reflected back to her. And for the audience, I hope and believe that it brought home some of the pain and terror of what has since been referred to as the 'witch hunt' of gay men and lesbians in the military over the past few decades.

One of the most powerful and memorable quotations from Vito's interview is when she tells of the time that she was called up in front of her commanding officers who showed her some love letters Vito had written. *"I thought, 'She's got evidence in front of her,' and in that spilt second it seemed better not to lie. To be called a liar would have seemed worse than being a lesbian to me."*

The 1967 Sexual Offences Act did not apply to the merchant

177

navy or to the armed services. One section of that act limited the application of the act to the civil arena, with homosexuality in the military remaining an offence under the 1955 Army and Air Force Acts and the 1957 Naval Discipline Act. It wasn't until 1999 that the ban on gays serving in the military was suspended after the Court of Human Rights declared it to be illegal. The court stated that the government's policy of sacking all known homosexuals from the armed forces was a breach of their human rights.

In this chapter we also hear from gay and lesbian police officers based in London, whom I interviewed for the Metropolitan Police film, *Queens' Evidence*. Kevin tells us (in his Scottish accent) what many gay men have long suspected: *"In those days everybody knew, judges knew, that police officers gilded the lily a bit just to get that bit extra. I'm not necessarily saying 'planting', but just to push it up the road a bit so that you would get a conviction."*

Kevin and Gamal have both given very open accounts in this chapter of being gay officers in the police and Carl tells us of a time when he courageously challenged homophobic comments made by other officers. In 1991 the Lesbian & Gay Police Association (LAGPA, later the Gay Police Association, GPA) was formed and, to give credit where it is due, the Met has become an organisation that goes to great lengths to show it wants to be gay-friendly – to its own staff and officers and to London's LGBT population.

CS

~

Interviews

The Armed Forces

VITO:
I left school at fifteen and got a job in a shop, then I joined the navy at seventeen. I had no education to speak of. I got the Wrens [Women's Royal Naval Service] magazine and the glamour of something like that was uncontrollable for me. I

liked the uniform of the Wrens, it looked better than the army or the air force. I liked the black and white. At that time it was so appealing but when I look back, it was obvious why I was doing it. The alternative was marriage, which was not a thought in my head even though I'd had boyfriends and been engaged, but in my heart of hearts I thought it was wrong, so joining the navy was the best thing that happened to me really. I was terrified because I hadn't really thought it through, and my mother was sort of hanging onto my legs on the train to stop me. She didn't want to lose me.

I spoke broad Geordie, nobody could understand a word I was saying and I'd never come across people who didn't speak Geordie. I had no particular skills and no training and of course then I got used to it and I learned a profession. I had opportunities I would never have dreamed of having in my life. I learned to shoot, to ride, to play badminton. I did helicopter jumps and gliding. Eventually I became a quarters petty officer and then I rose to the grand rank of chief petty officer which is the highest of the non-commissioned ranks.

I had my first relationship with a woman when I was twenty-one. I suppose we were a club within a club. It was like a subculture, the pinky rings were usually the telling factor. You used to wear a ring if you were gay. You wore a little signet ring with an onyx stone in it and it could be any colour. I mean, it wasn't guaranteed but we usually sussed each other out, and if we wanted each other to know we'd wear one of these rings. One of your partners would buy you one. You didn't usually buy your own.

We thought we were being really clever and hiding it all, but these other women knew. It's that gaydar stuff, isn't it, that takes one to know one? You weren't always right of course, you could make mistakes and it was dodgy to make mistakes. I think, within that subculture, people would ask questions and put enough information together before you asked. So life became quite rich in that respect because you felt you were part of an inner sanctum with people who understood you and shared your career.

You did four-year stints in the Wrens and when you got to

twelve you had to sign for your pension. I'd got to the eight and I'd signed up to do twelve and at the ten-year mark they found out I was a lesbian through a woman I'd had a relationship with. It was long since over but she'd got caught and she didn't do the decent thing and alert some of her friends that a witch hunt was on, because she was trying to deny it, and of course they had to then try and prove it. So they searched her things and found some letters of mine and there were quite a few people implicated. People had written to her, her friends, some had been her lovers. The first I knew about it was standing in front of the officer in charge and I could see copies of my letters that were written some time earlier, quite a few years ago, and she charged me with being a lesbian. So what do you do? I wasn't going to lie. I thought, "She's got evidence in front of her," and in that spilt second it seemed better not to lie. To be called a liar would have seemed worse than being a lesbian to me. She said, "Do you know what it means?" And I said yes I did.

I suppose I was in shock. I just couldn't believe it, really. It took a while to sink in but basically my career was at an end from that moment on. I'd got a really good service record and it obviously felt so grossly unfair because the premise behind this act is that you're at risk of sharing government secrets and breaching the Official Secrets Act. Well, the job I did had no access to any secrets but the girlfriend I was going out with at the time was working in Morse code in Whitehall. They didn't know about that, of course.

As soon as I found out, I kept away from my friends and so on and alerted them to the fact that they'd be investigated. Anyone I was with. So it was horrendous because I was then feeling isolated. I couldn't use my support systems without implication.

The witch hunt I was involved with went on for a long time. I was out in about four weeks but I retained some connection with some of the people and some of them had lied their way to keep their career and they were not happy because they were forever watched; and some people lost the ability for promotion. They lost their status, their character was in question. They were demoralised. I think I made the right choice actually, when I look back. At the time it didn't feel like that, because I was relatively destitute because I had no money as such.

When the witch hunt was on, it was horrendous because I was made to see a psychiatrist. You see, it was pathologised in those days, it was considered a psychiatric condition. They were looking for evidence to dismiss me. If they'd put a psychiatric assessment on me then they could dismiss me on 'services no longer required' or 'in ill health' or 'unfit for duty'. 'Services no longer required' could mean anything to a civilian employer, but you knew what it meant. I remember seeing the psychiatrist and I was in the waiting room. I was in Duchess of Kent barracks in Portsmouth and it was very high in this old Victorian block and I remember looking down into the parade ground and seeing somebody I knew was gay and knocking on the window trying to get their attention and realising, "Oh God, I'd better not do that, because if Sally waves to me she'll be implicated as well."

I can see myself, I was standing on the steps waiting for my taxi to take me to my bedsit in Earls Court, which was all I could afford, and just still in shock four weeks on. My uniform had been handed in. I'd had to do all these leaving rounds: you had to go to your pay department to hand back your pay book, your equipment and uniform department to hand back your uniform. It's like everything was taken away from you. There was tremendous shame involved in that. I wasn't out to my parents then and I felt so ashamed, I felt I had to lie, so I couldn't expect them to give me any support either... and of course I was out without a pension.

JACK:

At the age of eighteen I had to do two years' National Service. I'd already done two years working from the age of sixteen to eighteen when I worked in London in the rag trade in Mayfair. At one point in National Service the commanding officer interviewed me on day one and he said, "I see that in Civvy

Street you worked in the rag trade. Now you're not one of these nancy boys, are you?" And I said, "Sir?" Because at that time I had had no physical relationship with another person, male or female. Of course in the army none of this happened although there were two boys who I got to know very well who actually got out of doing National Service on the basis of being gay. I think they pushed it rather and became over-gay with all the associated mannerisms that were around in those days in the 1950s when none of this was legal.

EMMANUEL:

I wanted to do National Service because I wanted a flavour of life outside the village, with the potential for sexual adventure. It was terribly disappointing, but I did meet a man there who was gay. Although he never articulated this, he recognised me as being gay and I recognised him as being gay and we became good friends, although it was certainly a non-sexual relationship. Len came from a middle-class family and we just went to the theatre and cinema together. On one occasion he said, "Do you like going out with me?" and I said, "Yes I do," and he said, "Well, you know, people think I'm a bit odd." What he meant was a bit camp. I got terribly confused and blushed terribly because I felt he was saying something that was very difficult at this point in my life. Though really when I look back on it, he was being terribly nice. No-one had ever said it out loud or made it acceptable, so Len was really quite a revelation in my life.

I was in the air force near Stanford in Lincolnshire and in Stanford there was a toilet and I used to spend hours there every evening. Well, some evenings just hanging about and occasionally one would see people and I'd just run away. But again, there was this curious thing which was that one or two of the airmen in the air force I became very friendly with and I just loved controlling them, but I didn't have any sex in the air force.

I remember Len wrote me a letter saying he'd been

somewhere and met these people and that they were just "as camp as a row of tents" and I thought, "What does that mean?" But you knew what it meant.

CAROL:
A lot of the army girls were given shock treatment to make them straight so they went on the run and came to London or wherever to get away from it all. They had a terrible time. And if you had a girlfriend and they got to find out about it, they'd ship her up North and ship you down South and try and split it up that way.

ROS:
I had this friend who was in the army and she had a girlfriend who went down there banging on the doors and everything. My friend was pulled out and put in a cell and all her stuff was gone through and she had to leave, she was thrown out. They searched all her belongings, her letters from this woman. I think this woman was banging and demanding to see her girlfriend. I mean, can you imagine?

LEONARD:
There used to be merchant seamen... When the boats left England the whole crew got into drag, they said, and also these great liners. A lot of the butch people were cross-dressers. I wasn't in the navy but they came to London and said, "Where is it? Where's the drag?" Top sailors who used to want to get into women's clothes and often it was the very butch ones. Have you heard of Boogie Street in Singapore? It was a drag centre and the Royal Navy used to go there.

My big line is the army. A guardsman for eighteen years used to come here every Wednesday. You know the Horseguards? They go right back to the sixteenth century. They're all on the game in London, guards have always been available, not all of them, but lots of them. You met them in bars in those days. There were two bars in Knightsbridge, one was called The Paxton's Head. There was one in Soho, The Golden Lion. The one I knew worked for the royal family, his wife was a friend of Princess Diana when they married because he worked for Prince Charles by then. He was bisexual. But the funny thing about these people, they're not homosexual, but they go to gay bars. They're bisexual. I always have relationships with bisexuals. I don't like gays, I can't stand effeminate people. I much prefer virile men, but if you see them on the street you ignore them. You never acknowledged them in public.

REX:
Servicemen were around to be picked up in the Fifties, there's no doubt about that. Once, back in '53, it was coronation year, I was with a guy in Park Lane and a friend of his came out of The Dorchester and assumed that I was a guardsman – and I was insulted, because he assumed that his friend had picked up this guardsman. I was tall, I was pretty well built but I was insulted because, you know, because I was an actor, I wasn't a guardsman. After I walked away I realised that I could have got several quid out of this guy! Oh yes, guardsmen were terrible. I would have thought, in the majority of cases, I believe guardsmen were paid.

There was a guy I knew in the navy and he knew that if he came to London, nothing ever happened in the services, but if he came to London, on leave, he could get a free night's lodging as a serviceman. Any eighteen-, nineteen-year-old who was in the services.

JIMMY:
My landlady at Shepherds Bush knew that I was gay because she said to me, "I saw you bring two sailors back last night." I'd picked them up in Lyons Corner House in Charing Cross.

It was a huge place and it used to be open all night and

closed for one hour for cleaning up. Of course all the forces went there – because so many people came up to London when they were in the forces and that was the place to pick people up, if they'd got nowhere to go, and they got the train the next day.

I went with a guy who I met in a sauna bath, he had a car, and we took [the sailors] back to Shepherds Bush and they were, as I say, gay-friendly, and I had two bedrooms in that place. The next day I made dinner for them, and we used to go and have a drink at one of the pubs at Shepherds Bush and everything was all right. So it wasn't all doom and gloom!

The Police

KEVIN:
I joined on 3 January 1978 and went to Hackney. I would never, could never have told anybody there or any of my colleagues. I knew that if I had, I would have not fitted in. I would not have been allowed really to finish my probation and if you don't fit in, in the police culture, police officers have a highly imaginative and creative way of getting together and doing things to make you feel uncomfortable. It would have been property loss, things which would have been essential for me to do my job properly. I have absolutely no doubt in my mind that that's what they would have done, made it so uncomfortable for me that I would have had to leave.

There were times when I was on duty and I'd go to a cottage and if I was with somebody, and if I was able to swing round and see what was going on, fine, I started making a bit of a joke about it. So I would say things like, "Let's be having you." But some of my colleagues didn't like that 'cos a lot of times they would make up the evidence. But I wasn't the type of guy who would make up evidence. I mean, in those days everybody knew, judges knew, that police officers gilded the lily a bit just to get that bit extra. I'm not necessarily saying 'planting', but just to push it up the road a bit so that you would get a conviction.

I remember policing a Pride march twenty-four, twenty-five years ago, maybe one of the first Pride marches, and it ended in those days down behind the Royal Festival Hall. We were all sitting in these green buses, bored really, and I remember one guy sitting in the bus, he was one of these gobby guys, and when all the banners were being unfurled and folded and put away and whatnot, there was a Gay and Lesbian Teachers banner and this guy said, "Fucking Hell. Who would want that shower of fucking queer shit teaching your kids? I tell you, fucking Hitler had a good idea." And from the back of the bus there was an officer who was reading a paper – could have been the *Guardian*, I don't know – he said, "Oy, mouth. Shut the fuck up!" And the guy did. Now I'm not saying the guy who said that was gay. I'm not saying he has gay brothers or sisters, I'm not saying anything other than the fact that he found what that other guy was saying offensive. There's always going to be maybe somebody who objected but not many people would have been brave enough to say, "Oy!" Because it would have been, "Aye aye? You must be one of them!" It was quite difficult.

I remember one night being on duty as the custody sergeant, this was about 1983, and the back door swung open and in came two policemen with these two prisoners. One man, a middle-aged man in a suit, and the other one, a young lad, Glaswegian accent, and it was, "Get your hands off me."

I said, "Excuse me just a sec, that's enough, just take the cuffs off and stand there. Listen to what the officers are saying because they have to tell me the circumstances of you being arrested."

"It was all lies," he said.

I said, "Well, just a second."

Then the officer who brought them in said, "We were making our patrol round the outside of Russell Square and we heard a muffled talk and rummaging in the bushes so we went in and saw these two men here engaged in oral sex."

And I thought, "How could they be doing that and talking at the same time?"

"That's a lie!" the young one said. "Look at this thing! I would never be having any sex with him!"

OK fine, so, "Empty your pockets." He emptied his pockets and he had a bottle of poppers and KY Jelly, he may have had condoms. I said, "What's that for?"

"What?"

I said, "That gel?"

"It's for my hair. It gaise it the wet look."

So we eventually sorted that out and I think they were then charged and were going to go to court. Now the next day the chief superintendent, he was an old sweat, "Awright lads?" He came down and he said, "Sergeant Boyle, get over here!" He said, "What was this about these guys being charged last night? This mucking and fucking around in the gardens? Right, who were the arresting officers?"

So I told him.

"Go on that relief, brief them all, I don't want any of them... how dare they? Go into the bushes and parks? I'm not having any of that!"

And I thought, "Well, bloody hell, he's quite enlightened."

"Because I'll tell you why, because the bum bandits in those parks are judges and they're MPs and then the commissioner gets on to me and I've got nothing but fucking grief from the press. So tell them to fuck off and get some burglars!"

And I thought, brilliant! So I had to say to them all the next day: "Now listen, fellows, if any of you are out now patrolling, the chief superintendent does not want you to patrol Russell Square and similar places. I know it's easy bodies, but you need to get out there and find some burglars.

GAMAL:

I started off as a police officer in 1992 when I was twenty-eight years old, I started back then. I sat in the canteen and people wouldn't say racist remarks to me but I heard homophobic remarks all the time. Or Dale Winton was on the TV or something and there'd be, "Oh, that bloody poof's on the telly again." And the impact it had on me was: "Don't tell anybody."

I came from a very traditional African Muslim background

and I was the only son of my father, so the expectations of that were on me, that I was going to carry on the family name. I'm the one to give the family children and so I had that going on which was clashing with my sexual identity. I didn't come out till I was forty, so up until then I was in this place of real denial. I think I joined the police to hide behind the uniform. I didn't have to be me when I was in uniform.

I didn't socialise as much with people because, you know, often times if there were team weddings or team events where people would bring their partners then I'd have a reason not to go, but if it was something like a drink after work or a leaving do then I would go. But outside of work it was lonely because I didn't have a partner, I didn't have anything like that. I was scared to have a partner in case somebody found out.

There was a gay couple in the area I worked in, and this gay couple I remember used to have domestic arguments all the time. We'd get called there quite a few times and every time we were called there, whoever was going there, it would be like, "Watch your back, boys!" and "Stand with your bums against the wall," and "Handbags at dawn again." On the way there it was always taken as a joke.

There was a public toilet that was known for cruising and cottaging, and operations were set up on this toilet all the time and it was, "Let's go and get the faggots," and stuff like that. There were public toilets on the ground that we used to do a lot of operations on, hiding in the ceilings. You'd put a roof in the toilet, one of these false ceilings, so there was the ceiling there and the toilets underneath, and people would climb up into the roof space and there'd be a little hole. Somebody would hide in the ceiling and build a radio and we'd have unmarked cars and plain-clothes officers hiding around. It was also about looking for the young, freshest-looking probation officer to go in and be bait. You had six teams and there were five shifts so there was always a team that was a spare team, a rolling spare team, and that team maybe as a project for their week on operational policing, that would be their week to go and do the toilets or whatever operation would come up, but inevitably it was to do the toilets. I just took it in my stride and I suppose the only thing was that I felt if I didn't do it, it would draw attention.

CARL:

I joined the police as a traffic warden in August 1981 and I thought, "This job, I'm not going to let anyone bully me about being gay. I'll come out, I'll be open." Once they knew that, the bullying started and I was up in the controller's office every now and then being bullied. "You've got a dirty collar." Then I became an acting supervisor 'cos they had to let me, but when I applied for the board they said, "Your name's not on the list, Mr Johnson." They always called you Mr This or Mrs That. I said, "Why not?"

"You're not suitable." They didn't say it was because I was gay but I knew it was.

I said, "Look, all my compatriots in the job are all getting promoted above me." I said, "I've got experience."

But they just said, "You're not suitable."

Eventually I got moved to a police station as a traffic warden in 1994 and I can remember one day I applied for overtime because there was a Gay Pride march, so I applied for the overtime to basically stand by the gates and advise people: "What gate is for the beer tent?" "Oh, Gate 8. Up the other end." "What gate will we need for the show, or the gay discos?" "You need Gate C or you can go through there but it's a longer walk through the park." That was my job to sort of guide the public.

Well, I went in like I was supposed to, 8am, to start the shift, get my briefing sheets, how they're going to police it. I went into the canteen and my manager, she said to me, "Carl, it's going to be a long day, have an hour's break to start off with. Have a big breakfast and a cup of coffee. Set yourself up 'cos you're going to be at the gates, it could go on to, well, probably ten o'clock at night, but you're on overtime."

So I marched down the corridor to the canteen and there were these plain-clothes police in that area, going to look out for pickpockets in the park. 'Cos in the summer they had shorts,

I think it was July or August it goes on, and they're wearing trainers. Some of them looked just like gay blokes. T-shirt with 'Guinness' on, although you could see by the haircuts that any gay person could spot them a mile off that they were police. Do you know what I mean? The haircut at the back and some of them had 'Stonewall' on their shirts to try and fit in.

So all the coppers were there in the canteen, plain clothes with their cups of tea and their breakfast, and one of them who'd been on a recce to find if anyone's arriving yet, he's coming back to the police station and he walked into the canteen and goes, "Awright, Dave?"

And this other guy says, "What's it like down there?"

Then he goes, "Ha ha ha, fucking load of poofs!"

I thought, "That's it. I'm not going to put up with that." So I went *bash* with my cup on the saucer, stood up, pushed the chair away, walked out. Got a lift up to the third floor where the chief inspector works who is in charge. Went down the corridor, knocked on his door. He said, "Come in," in his gruff manner and he was a very tall thin guy with black hair and I remember he had National Health black spectacles and he goes, "Yes? Your name?"

I said, "My name's Carl Johnson."

He said, "And you're in the traffic warden department?"

"Yes that's right." 'Cos he could see from my uniform.

So he said, "What's the problem?"

I said, "The problem is, sir, that one of your plain-clothes constables down in the canteen has just made homophobic remarks about the Pride situation. He's been down there for a recce to see how many people he estimates will be turning up down there. He says it's quite peaceful but he said, 'What a load of fucking poofs!'" I said, "I'm not having it."

"Oh well, Carl," he says, "it is a Gay Pride day. He is dealing with gay people."

I said, "Well, that's not how he should be dealing with it, is it?" I said, "I am gay myself and I will not put up with it."

He went bright red. This is the chief inspector, three stars, he went bright red.

He said, "OK, what does he look like?"

I said, "He's the guy with balding black hair, a Guinness T-shirt on."

"I know the one. I'll have a word with him."

I said, "Thank you very much, Inspector. And don't say, 'It's a Gay Pride day, so what do you expect?' 'Cos I don't expect that, I expect the police to be polite, OK?"

"OK, OK, Carl." And he ushered me out and I thought, "Well, I've done my bit."

A lot of gay people don't like me, especially the older gay people. They say I shouldn't have joined the police 'cos I know how the police have treated gay people. I'm a traitor. To them I'm a traitor joining the police, you know? They've been nicked themselves for cottaging and all that and they say, "So what are you doing in the police? And if you're a policeman, what are you doing coming to a gay pub?" So really, if I'm in that job, I can't win.

11

CLASSROOM CLOSET:
THE TEACHING PROFESSION

Several of the people I interviewed for the play *Gateway to Heaven* had worked as teachers. I hadn't known this before I met them and it made me think about the large numbers of lesbians and gay men who have always worked in that profession. Looking at the extracts in this chapter helps to remind us why there is still so much fear of coming out in teaching. Whilst many large businesses, financial companies, health authorities, governmental agencies and councils appear keen to improve and publicise their ratings regarding how well they treat their LGBT employees, schools and colleges lag far behind. This is partly because teachers do not come out in large numbers, or press for rights concerning equality in the workplace, because of their fear that a disgruntled child or parent might use their sexuality against them. Gerard explains this point quite powerfully by saying: *"There was always the possibility that at some time you would have to take an unpopular action against a child and children will lash out with the nearest weapon that comes to hand."*

Gay and lesbian teachers who have devoted their entire lives to the profession will often not want to risk revealing their sexuality if their career might be jeopardised and the benefit of their work thereby undermined or negated. This is unfortunately still the case today and has been for as long as many contributors in this book can recall. Bob C describes an incident in the 1970s when he went along to a meeting of the National Union of Teachers (NUT), in which he was active, to discuss the issue of a gay colleague who had been dismissed. He says: *"Hackney was terribly left-wing and they were saying, 'Um... we're not sure about this...' I mean, they would have supported the general strike in Bolivia but actually to support a gay teacher in ILEA [Inner London Education Authority] was more difficult."*

This reluctance to address and advance lesbian and gay rights in the teaching profession is clearly because of the teachers' close involvement with children. Sadly many lesbian and gay teachers are still held hostage by bigoted people who assert that they might somehow either influence the children's sexuality or put the children at some sort of sexual risk. As Gregory M. Herek (professor of psychology at the University of California at Davis) writes:

"Members of disliked minority groups are often stereotyped as presenting a danger to the majority's most vulnerable members. Jews in the Middle Ages were accused of murdering Christian babies in ritual sacrifices. Black men in the United States were often lynched after being falsely accused of raping white women."[1]

Similarly lesbians and gay men have often been portrayed as a threat to children. Herek adds, however, that empirical research shows gay or bisexual men are no more likely than heterosexual men to molest children. This is not to argue that homosexual and bisexual men never molest children but there is no scientific basis for asserting that they are more likely than heterosexual men to do so.

It is not only men in teaching who are seen as a threat to children. Unmarried women teachers have also had to bear the weight of historical prejudice. Alison Oram, from the Lesbian History Group, points out that during the interwar years in Britain, the perceived image of the spinster teacher suffered an increasingly negative change, resulting in the stereotype of an embittered, thwarted, sexually frustrated or deviant woman.[2] She also reminds us that the sexual threat that spinster teachers were seen to pose cannot be disentangled from the economic threat that they presented to men.

These kinds of prejudice towards both lesbians and gay men contribute to the continuing difficulty that so many teachers have in feeling able to come out. In other professions that have begun to accept and embrace their LGBT staff, employees who can be themselves and not have to hide their sexuality are able to flourish in the workplace and thereby offer more to the organisation in return. Seventy years ago, no-one would have dreamed that people could be openly gay in professions such as the army, the navy and the police, as they are. Legally, of course, gay and lesbian teachers are allowed to be out, but the reality is that many of them still choose to hide their sexuality.

In the same way that, at long last, some gay rights campaigners are endeavouring to seek out and support gay men in sports such as rugby and football and to address homophobia in those areas, it is clear that a similar amount of work and attention is still needed to help and support lesbians and gay men in the teaching profession.

CS

~

Interviews

GERARD:

What I found, being a teacher, was I then began to have almost two lives: one where I was able to develop friends and a relationship but that had to be separated off from my work, and at work I had to disguise what I was really doing, so that was a two-sided thing that I found till I retired.

There was always the possibility that at some time you would have to take an unpopular action against a child and children will lash out with the nearest weapon that comes to hand. So they will either lash out with a name or else they might say that you have done something which you haven't done. So there are only a few brave souls who are out, mainly in secondary education.

BOB H:

When I started work at Sutton Grammar School for Boys in the Seventies, there were gay teachers but no-one was openly gay, not in those days. I recall the gay scene, you worked during the week, Monday to Friday, and then you partied heavily Friday to Sunday evening and then went back to work again. So you sort of came out of the closet at the weekends.

In 1980, when I moved to a big head of science job in a London school, then I was out to staff, but there were a few teachers out. Paul Patrick, who was quite a big character, a gay activist, who died recently, was an out teacher. So I was out to staff in 1980 in another boys' school and then in about 1983, or possibly 1984, I came out to the pupils. I was a senior teacher in a big amalgamated school and people were saying, "Oh, it's Gay Pride Week, we're doing equal opportunities at the school, can you speak at the assembly?" Staff knowing I was gay. So I said, "Well, yes I can speak but what am I going to say? I can't get up and talk about gay rights and this and that and the other and knowing I'm gay and not come out." So I said to the head and the chair of the governors: "Is it all right if I come out at assembly?" And they said, "OK." That was brilliant!

It's like one of those memories you have in your mind where you will never forget it. I mean you've got twelve, fourteen hundred kids there, you've got sixty staff all sat there fussing around. It's a Gay Pride assembly, everyone's yawning, out comes a senior teacher with the chair of the governors and we said we're going to do this and then I said: "You might wonder why I'm talking about all this, well it's 'cos I'm gay myself!" And at that point it was like someone had put fifty thousand volts through all the seating. Every kid went *wump!* And all the staff stopped doing their crosswords and looked up in total shock and then after that it all settled down a bit, it was interesting.

BOB C:

In about '72, '73, I got involved in the Gay Teachers and that was quite a big influence in terms of supporting teachers who wanted to be openly gay and to do stuff in schools and so on. And there was a friend of mine, John Warburton, who believed ILEA when they said they were supportive of gay teachers and he came out to some of his pupils, in a girls' school actually, but they still managed to sack him and he was a kind of *cause célèbre* for a while, that was about '74, I think. He got a lot of support from people like the Gay Teachers Group. That was, I suppose, one of the ways I became involved in my union as a gay man and I discovered that to try and persuade the unions to support a gay teacher, even though he had been sacked, was not straightforward at all. I remember going with him once to an NUT meeting in Hackney, which was terribly left-wing, and they were saying, "Um... we're not sure about this..." I mean, they would have supported the general strike in Bolivia but actually to support a gay teacher in ILEA was more difficult. But it was a very important learning process and a lot of the union activists did learn from that experience.

I think it was easier for me in that I worked in an FE college so all our students were over the age of sixteen and it was a matter of luck that I happened to land up in a very progressive kind of college. I was the only openly gay person on the staff and I suspect that some of my colleagues found it awkward, but because of the kind of place it was, they didn't make life awkward for me. I mean, I certainly had a much better experience than some colleagues in other colleges who faced a lot of opposition. I was out at work and I'd set up the gay group in my union, which was NATFHE [National Association of Teachers in Further and Higher Education] eventually. There were just two of us and we used to lobby the annual conferences and things like that.

We set up our group in 1974. There were several gay groups being set up in public sector trade unions at that time, nurses, social workers, but they were really, really tiny, two or three people in these unions of thousands of people. What I tried to do was to get the question of Gay Liberation on the agenda of the union and so we tried to get resolutions discussed at annual conferences. It was very important for us to get those kinds of things on the agenda so that they were discussed and we worked with a left-wing pressure group called Rank and File and they did become quite supportive of us. But there were all these people who were lecturers and teachers baying and shouting at us sometimes. I remember one year, we always gave out leaflets at the conference sessions about the fact that the gay group was there, and people were sort of screwing up the leaflets and throwing them on the ground. I really think they would have been more tolerant if we'd been the National Front. It was really quite hateful.

One of the events I do feel quite proud of, in 1980 the union held its conference in Scarborough, and Scarborough at that time was refusing to hold CHE conferences there, so we decided that NATFHE shouldn't be holding conferences there, and several organisations were boycotting Scarborough's conference facilities. We thought they shouldn't have gone there but they did, so we produced stickers saying "Glad to be Gay in Scarborough", and we got large numbers of delegates to wear these stickers around the place and that was good for people as an act of solidarity. Some of them were astonished to find that when they went into a bar with these stickers on, the barman would refuse to serve them. It was good just to let them experience that.

The high point was when the mayor came to make one of those speeches at the beginning of the conference. A couple of us were up in the balcony with a Gay Teachers banner which we unfurled and then various people in the audience sang 'Glad to Be Gay' and it wasn't street theatre, but it was a conference version of street theatre. Very powerful. And the mayor was completely staggered by this but I think the NATFHE officials were even more staggered that this could happen within their midst. After that NATFHE recognised the concerns of lesbian and gay men as concerns they had to take on board a bit. For example, they never went back to Scarborough. There were also conferences at one time in Jersey, where homosexuality was still illegal, and NATFHE began to talk about going to Jersey and then when they realised what the situation was there they didn't go. But you could then have discussions at conference.

People who were being harassed at work did get support more easily. But the group was set up in '74 and we're talking about over ten years. An important conference was in 1988, about the time Clause 28 became law, and we had a conference resolution opposing Clause 28, committing the union to take action. The conference was completely united against Clause 28; people applauding gay speakers and all that sort of thing, it was a very different atmosphere.

JEAN:
During the custody case and when my ex-husband was beating me up, my colleagues at school knew and were very supportive. I thought, "I'm going to have to go and see the head teacher," because I knew that Frank was going to go in there and tell her about me being gay and of course, being PE, it was even worse because you're so vulnerable. So I went in and told her, but she's not stupid. I'd been to school with black eyes, sunglasses in the middle of winter. She knew I'd been going through a bad time. She lent me money for my deposit for my flat, which I paid her back, because she knew I was desperate. I said, "My husband's going to come in and tell you that I'm a lesbian." And she was fine: "No-one's going to be victimised on this staff, so don't worry." So, I was lucky in that situation. It was at a time there was that geography teacher, he'd mentioned that he'd been on a gay march somewhere or other, and he lost his job. I remember there were lots of marches about it.

12

HIV/AIDS: A TURNING POINT

The appearance of HIV/AIDS in the early 1980s sent shockwaves across the world, from Africa to America to Europe and back again. One of the impacts of this disease was that there was a setback in western society in the level of tolerance and understanding that gay men had been experiencing, gradually, over the previous decades. In the British tabloid press, AIDS was the subject of many headlines and caused great alarm among the public. In some newspapers, the prejudice was obvious. Haemophiliacs were seen as the 'innocent victims' of AIDS whereas gay men and drug-users were seen as having brought the disease upon themselves.[1] The fear of AIDS encouraged the fire brigade to ban the kiss of life, and caused holidaymakers to cut their holiday short for fear of contracting AIDS from an HIV-positive (at the time called 'HTLV-III-positive') passenger on the Queen Elizabeth 2 cruise ship.[2] A nine-year-old positive haemophiliac was allowed to attend the local school, but some of the pupils were kept home by anxious parents.[3]

Bob C tells us: *"Once I counted up the number of men I know who have died, and it's at least twenty and most of them are either my age, or would have been my age, or younger. The youngest I can think of was twenty-four. He was diagnosed and within three weeks he was dead."* I think that Bob's recollections bring home the point about how quickly men became infected while the government did nothing but create fear and spread negative propaganda.

But Emmanuel suggests that AIDS was also a turning point for gay men, because they started talking about gay sex. This led to education about, and fuller awareness of, the issues surrounding gay sexuality, for both themselves and society in general. He says: *"I think it completely changed the landscape in lots of different ways. One was that it politicised gays in a way and it politicised the whole nation in a way that had not been politicised before."*

There might be an argument then that, in common with the 1954 Montagu Case, the advent of AIDS shows that sometimes a terrifying and appalling event can cast light on the experiences of a partially hidden sector of society and even result in outcomes that help the struggle towards equal rights. Gill observes, *"It was AIDS that changed the schism between lesbians and gay men that had occurred in the late Seventies."*

By the end of 1984 there had been 108 cases of AIDS and 46 deaths in the UK. At the end of 2010, 30 million people worldwide were living with HIV.[4]

Many of us have experienced the loss of somebody in our life to this cruel disease and might be thinking of them as they read through the extracts below, but I would personally like to dedicate this chapter to Andrew.

CS

~

Interviews

EMMANUEL:
One had heard murmurs about AIDS in '82, '83, about this awful mysterious disease which was affecting men – through mostly Kaposi's sarcoma at that point – in America. There was a club in the West End called Subway which was in the basement of a building in Leicester Square, which was a big club, this was in about 1978, and was this a good thing or a bad thing? We had to discuss it in Gay Left. Generally the consensus was that it was a good thing because it was opening up another world

of possibilities for gay men. The arguments against it being a good thing were commercialism, exploitation, a particular formation of sexuality around the body, around pleasure and entertainment, which had no political dimension, but to some that was just an old-fashioned view as to what politics was about.

I remember that Subway had a back room, so you could have sex in this dark space, the whole thing was terribly cruisy and it was terribly exciting and completely new in one sense. There had always been tiny little clubs where all sorts of things went on, one or two down the Kings Road you used to go to, but Subway was really quite different 'cos it was big, it was in the centre of town and somebody said to me, "That's where you get AIDS," and I thought, "Oh my God, that's probably true." There were all sorts of theories in the early days – that it came through sniffing poppers, that was one very common theory – but nobody quite knew, obviously. But it didn't seem to me as if that was likely, it seemed to me to do with the number of contacts you were having sexually, it didn't make any sense otherwise, so after that I was really rather careful, fortunately, so far. That was quite early on and then a friend of mine died two or three years later and one became aware of it, very graphically. When he died, and that was in '85, and they still couldn't identify it, it was still very difficult to identify medically although one knew what it was.

I think it completely changed the landscape in lots of different ways. One was that it politicised gays in a way and it politicised the whole nation in a way that had not been politicised before. For the first time people were talking about fucking, and gay men fucking, and talking about gay sex in a way that had just not been possible before. All this came through AIDS and the realisation that to control it you had to do certain things, you either had to not do it or you had to wear a condom or all these other things, but it was a discussion.

There was so much ignorance and fear at the beginning and it was the time of the government's "Ignorance Is Death" campaign, which was just appalling, 'cos you don't die of ignorance, you die of disease. It was just alarmist and unhelpful and they said, "Everyone's at risk," and not everyone is at risk. You're only at risk if you do certain things and all that misinformation was around.

But the government on the whole did move slowly towards a much more sensible and a much more coherent policy and it did change the political landscape. People did become more politicised, but it was around an issue, it wasn't around what we would have called politics, but of course it is politics, because it is the way we control or define or look at our own body. With AIDS, I think there was the idea that you had to raise awareness about what this thing was all about and at the same time you had to deal with the behaviour and the prejudice.

BOB C:
I remember with the Chilean boyfriend I had in 1972, having a conversation about what we'll be doing ten years from now. What we would be doing is facing up to AIDS. It was certainly nothing that any of us conceived of at all. It was incredibly difficult to deal with. I suppose in the early Eighties it appeared when I was into casual sex, so I was very much in the high-risk group that was becoming infected. I've never tested for all different kinds of reasons: didn't need to, scared, and then as time has gone on... I don't look like I'm losing weight, but the reasons for not testing have changed over the years.

At the beginning it was all kinds of denial. I remember once meeting a man in a disco and he was a Liberian and he'd been educated in America, his father was a diplomat. He sounded American and one of the pieces of advice at the time was "Don't sleep with Americans". But I knew it would be all right to sleep with him because he was a Liberian. In terms of everything except his passport he was an American but I convinced myself that it would be all right.

I think AIDS politicised a lot of gay men who otherwise had not been political at all. Once I counted up the number of men I know who have died, and it's at least twenty and most of them are either my age, or would have been my age, or younger. The youngest I can think of was twenty-four. He was diagnosed and within three weeks he was dead, and he was politically active. It was like he didn't have the capacity to transfer the struggle he brought to his politics to his own life. He just gave up. And I say *at least* twenty because sometimes people have just moved away and I don't know if they're alive or dead. My circle has not been decimated in the way some people's circles have. I knew one man in Tottenham and he was the last of quite a close circle he belonged to, of eight or ten men. He was the last one alive, he's now dead. I know a number of people who are HIV positive but obviously it's different now from the guy who died in three weeks. People now have got a whole new set of opportunities to access treatment and turn around their lives.

There were lots of gay men who benefited from the fact that there was a gay movement, and a big blossoming of the gay scene, particularly in the late Seventies, early Eighties, who didn't really have any kind of politics at all. This was the kind of life that they'd wanted and they could have it. I think for many of them AIDS was a complete mind-fuck in what was happening. It completely blew the world away.

I suppose some men never got over the tragedy of it really but some did and some became very committed in self-help activities, running drop in centres and producing newsletters and I think that that self-help tradition was one of the most important things that came out of that mid Eighties period. It was extremely difficult to get support from anyone at all at that time so I suppose they began to realise that they were not just people who felt desire for other men, they were part of a group in society and like any group in society, if you work together, you can get things that you don't get if you don't work together. Among some men who had not been politically conscious there was a consciousness about what it meant to be a gay man.

When AIDS started I was teaching and I tried to make sure that HIV was brought onto the curriculum of the college where I was teaching. I was also for a time a volunteer on [London

Lesbian and Gay] Switchboard. People were just absolutely freaked out by the kind of calls they would get. You would get people phoning up and really not knowing about transmission at all and whether or not they were at risk of being infected. Once I'd got over the denial thing I found it easy to absorb the principles of safer sex but even after quite sensible things had been published in the tabloid press, you would get calls from men who had just no idea about what was going on. They'd be terrified of touching a door handle but they'd be having sex without condoms. Sometimes people would call up and they had never talked about sex. They didn't know how to say, "This is what I'm doing." Sometimes there was all sorts of stuff coming out, real confusion about their sexuality, about their practice, about HIV transmission, about homophobia, about how it was all right to have sex with their wives without condoms, all kinds of stuff that was going on.

Some people at Switchboard were very much in danger of being burnt out by it. I remember one person telling me about a call he had on a shift he was on, from somebody who was Scottish going back to Inverness. He was twenty-four and he'd never come out to his family, and this is mid Eighties when there weren't any effective treatments around, and he'd been diagnosed as having AIDS. So he had to go back to Inverness to tell his family first of all that he's gay and then that he's got a terminal illness. My friend who answered the phone was really good and a good person to get but he was really struggling. How can you be cheery under those kind of circumstances?

PETER B:
I think it hit slowly. I was working at *Gay News* and I was aware of this 'gay men's cancer', I think it was called. I was aware of two friends in the States, who are now dead, one on the West Coast and one in New York who got stuck there. Then by 1982 I'd joined what became *Gay Times* and we were aware that there was this 'gay plague' as everybody was referring to it at this point, and I don't know how much we started to

worry about it until we realised that people we knew were ill. Retrospectively, we knew people that probably died from AIDS long before anyone knew anything about gay cancer. They had mysterious wasting diseases that no-one knew what it was and then suddenly lots of people had HIV, well, more full-blown AIDS, and people were dying.

There was a point when I seemed to be endlessly writing obituaries, endlessly writing eulogies for funerals and endlessly at funerals almost to a degree where I used to say, "Thank God I can write." Because you write about their life and it gives you a chance to intellectualise, and if I hadn't been able to write, it would have been much more unbearable, or if I hadn't been articulate and been able to talk to other people who were articulate. In a curious kind of way it went away. Well, it hasn't gone away, but all of the people in my generation or in my social circle who were going to die are all dead.

TAZ:
I actually think that there was a morality that was created by AIDS which the gay community has absorbed without really analysing it properly, and now we've created a class of people who practise protected sex and people who don't. If you are a protected sex person, you are wonderful, wonderful, wonderful! If you don't, you are promiscuous.

BOB H:
I had a general attitude towards the police. They were all scum in my view. That was probably because of the way gay people were treated by them. I mean, one incident in particular, when would that have been? It was between 1980 and 1983, early Eighties, AIDS time, there was a small disco opened up in Lewisham, quite near the school, nice little gay disco, Frolics, I think it was called. Not quite in the West End, in Lewisham. And I remember the police, the borough commander at the time, or the district commander, he decided he wasn't having

that on his patch. It was a jolly little thing. It was only on a Friday and Saturday, and we had a brilliant time, we took straight members of staff down there and all bopped away but there was a campaign in the papers: "We don't want this here, shut it down."

Then the police raided it one night. I wasn't there but we certainly heard about it. The owners knew they were going to raid it and shut it down 'cos of, supposedly, neighbour noise and whatnot. But the thing that stuck in my mind, and still does, was that the police came in there wearing washing-up gloves and anything else they could get. It looked as if some had got surgical gloves and if they couldn't find them had gone and got Marigold gloves out of the janitor's cupboard. So they're all piling in. It was disgusting! That was their attitude though, at the time, that you might catch AIDS from gay men. So people were removed as if they were vermin and that annoyed me then and still annoys me now. It was all down to ignorance.

GRIFF:
If the police raided a club they would go in with their Marigold gloves on, or whatever make they are, 'cos they were going to be asking people about the back rooms and what state they were in and inspecting them and things. So they went in and this was the big thing and they might be wearing them when perhaps they shouldn't have been. They were overreacting to perhaps what the job was. It might be that they were in a bookshop, perhaps, the general public were going in there but because it was a gay bookshop they might wear gloves. That's an example, I'm not sure they did that. But from what I could see that could be an overreaction, going into clubs with back bars and those sorts of places and one could argue that it was homophobic and there was probably no suggestion of AIDS or HIV.

JEFFREY:
Even nurses had full barrier protection with people with HIV and AIDS and you'd have to put a mask on and one of these plastic pinnies before going in to see someone with AIDS and that's what the nurses did, and the doctors. But there was a lot of paranoid fear of HIV at that stage, even in the community itself.

I think the Eighties was quite a dark period, culturally, politically and so on, and AIDS accentuated a feeling that the world was against us, and Section 28 of course was crucially important in confirming that.

GILL:
I think it was AIDS that changed the schism between lesbians and gay men that had occurred in the late Seventies. In a way I think it was necessary for... I can't say 'the lesbian movement', 'cos it's not that... but for women to go through that sense of anger, which was to be angry at men in general whether they were gay or straight or whatever, but just to sort of go through that quite extreme stuff and then come back to something that was more sensible. I do think that AIDS affected it, because I think people started to realise that, particularly with the anti-AIDS backlash, I think people started to come back together again as men and women, lesbians and gay men.

13

WE LIVED TO TELL THE TALE:
REFLECTIONS

In several of my interviews I asked the contributors how they thought that attitudes towards lesbians and gay men had changed over the years and whether they felt society in general had moved on sufficiently regarding gay rights or there was still work to be done. There has been a significant increase in legislation supporting lesbian and gay rights in the last fifteen or so years, mainly produced under the Labour government, and some of the contributors expressed the view that the bulk of the work had now been achieved. But others were a little more cautious, such as Sharley, who spoke about how, as a Jew in Nazi Germany, she *"experienced how quickly prejudices can be fed to rational human beings, because it's always easier to blame somebody"*.

Sharley reminds us, if we still need reminding, that it doesn't take much for social opinion to turn and victims to be sought and blamed for things that are going wrong in a society. It would be dangerous for lesbians and gay men to become at all complacent with the advances that have been gained. Achievements by liberation movements can easily slide – I would argue that the gains made by the feminist movement in the 1970s and '80s were never sufficiently secured in western society and that there has been a backsliding of women's rights in the workplace and the home – not to mention all the countries where basic equal rights for women have still to be achieved.

Jeffrey suggests that the introduction of Section 28 (also known as Clause 28) was part of the reason that gay men and lesbians were galvanised into fighting for and securing further basic civil rights. In 1983 the *Daily Mail* reported that a copy of a book entitled *Jenny Lives with Eric and Martin*, which portrayed a little girl living with her father and his male partner, had been provided in a school library run by the Labour-controlled Inner London Education Authority. In a climate of Thatcherite homophobia, fuelled by the increase of HIV/AIDS in Britain, the Tory government's response to the publication appeared on 24 May 1988 in the form of Section 28 of the Local Government Act. This act added an amendment which stated that a local authority "shall not intentionally promote homosexuality or publish material with the intention of promoting homosexuality" or "promote the teaching in any maintained school of the acceptability of homosexuality as a pretended family relationship". The possible implications of such an act were seen by some as quite threatening to a democracy. I recall hearing of libraries in certain local authorities who feared stocking any books that had ever been written by any lesbian or gay man, for fear of prosecution.

Echoing the backlash against the Montagu Case of 1954, Section 28 produced a regalvanisation of lesbian and gay groups at grass-roots level, as well as through the parliamentary lobbying group Stonewall, against what was seen by many as an unnecessary and retrograde political act. In 1990 the group Outrage! was formed at a meeting on 10 May 1990 as a queer rights direct action group. One of its four principal founders was the human rights activist Peter Tatchell.

Opinion in society is always a difficult thing to gauge but it would seem that at this point much of Britain's population were more accepting of homosexuality than the law and the government appeared to be, and certainly by the early to mid 1990s the attitude of the general public towards homosexuality appeared to have softened significantly.

Gay Pride marches had become more celebratory events than politicised protests. The police appeared increasingly relaxed in their attitudes towards the gay men and lesbians at the annual London Pride gatherings. Or perhaps the Met's reduction in aggressive policing allowed the marchers to feel more in a mood to celebrate than demonstrate.

It is quite probable that the change in attitude towards LGB people by the police had a knock-on effect on the way society in general viewed homosexuality. Val mentions how moved she was by the visible signs of change: *"When the police came in their uniform on Pride, that really got to me, it made me cry the first time I saw it, just because I thought, what a long way we'd come."*

It took the tragic murder of Stephen Lawrence, and the pitifully incompetent police investigation which followed, to lead, in turn, to the Macpherson Report of 1999, which was to famously term the Met "institutionally racist". Many officers within the police service itself, as well as outside commentators, have since argued that it was as a result of that report that the police then began to focus on lesbians and gay men as being one of the many and varied communities in London which they had a duty to try to understand and engage with. The Metropolitan Police have clearly made a concerted effort to change their ways and attitudes with regard to LGBT people and, as mentioned previously, were recently so keen to educate their officers that they commissioned my training film about LGBT history. As well as the police service there are an increasing number of employers in both the public and private sector who pride themselves on becoming increasingly supportive of their LGBT staff.

By the late 1990s, with the arrival of a Labour government, social attitudes in Britain became noticeably more accepting than they had ever been towards lesbians and gay men. When the age of consent was equalised to sixteen, under the Sexual Offences (Amendment) Act of 2000, and civil partnerships were introduced in 2005, it seemed to some that there could be no going back. But it would do us no harm to remember Sharley's words of caution.

This final chapter is a collection of extracts from the contributors discussing when and how they found that change and a degree of tolerance had finally come about in our society – something many of them had never expected to see in their lifetimes. From conducting interviews I have found that older lesbians and gay men have often spent a great deal of time thinking, not only about their own sexual orientation, but also about society's attitude towards them. Consequently they have a combination of the experience that comes with age, a vast store of wisdom and a depth of understanding around this particular matter that will greatly benefit, educate and enlighten any person, young or old, gay or straight, who chooses to listen.

CS

~

Interviews

JEFFREY:

I feel that the ice began to melt in the early Nineties and that was the climax of what we saw as a reaction to Section 28. Thatcher represented a sort of social conservatism and John Major attempted to be more liberal – and remember he invited Ian McKellen to Downing Street in the early Nineties? And I did begin to feel that things were beginning to relax. In 1994, of course, there was a big debate, the first debate really since the Sixties, about changing the law and reducing the age of consent from twenty-one to eighteen, and there was a big mobilisation around that, so homosexuality was being much more openly discussed in the early Nineties because of our political movement. Stonewall was then established, sort of leading the way politically and lobbying and so on and beginning to develop skills in bridging the gap between the community and the political leadership. But I think it was more than just John Major being a bit more liberal or a bit wetter than Thatcher. I really think that what's going on is a much more profound change. From 1967 on there was no change in the law except in the wrong direction, as with Section 28. But nevertheless our sense of ourselves, our sense of identity, our sense of community had been developing almost like an underground stream and although at first AIDS seemed a disaster to that, in practice it brought a new energy, I think, into gay movement activities in fighting against that backlash, and then of course Section 28, which was a tremendously mobilising thing.

So the gay movement, which at the beginning of the Eighties had seemed to have reached a new low, by the late Eighties was quite energetic. It wasn't a particularly militant gay movement. I mean, there were militant groupings and there was Peter Tatchell's work with Outrage! and so on, as well as what was happening with Stonewall, but I think the crucial shift is that by the early Nineties there were literally hundreds of thousands of people who weren't particularly political but who were prepared to stand up and be open about their gayness. I think it's that openness about gayness. Coming out is in some ways seen as old-fashioned now, but actually being open and relaxed about one's gayness in public is absolutely crucial to changing attitudes.

VAL:
When the police came in their uniform on Pride, that really got to me, it made me cry the first time I saw it, just because I thought, what a long way we'd come that they could actually come on the march with us, and that was lovely.

BOB C:
By the mid Eighties the climate in the Labour party began to change around lesbian and gay issues and we managed to set up a unit in Haringey. But there was quite a backlash from various religious and right-wing groups who encouraged a climate of violence. I remember seeing a car that a gay councillor was in being attacked by a man with an iron bar. At that time we felt we were really under siege.

I think every gay man of my age has been beaten up at least once.

CAROL:

I was beaten up in Earls Court. My girlfriend and I were walking down Earls Court Road and I just got attacked from the back. *Bang bang bang!* I learnt from that you don't fight back, you can't. It's impossible, because if you fought back it gave you more opportunity to be hit again, and it had happened to lots of gay men in drag so I just kept on walking. But it made you think about yourself. Wherever you went wearing drag was a problem, for work, for accommodation. When I see women in drag today I think, "God, if only you knew what it was like in the Sixties," and well, before then, it must have been even worse.

LINDA:

It's in our power as citizens to do something about a social order that says it's acceptable to treat someone less favourably because of the colour of their skin or because of who they sleep with. That to me remains politically and morally wrong. Now, the question is how do you get from where you are to where you want to be?

By action, by being involved, by making things different.

ROS:

I'll tell you when I think a big change came and it was when the butch and the femme became sort of one in appearance, that must have been in the Eighties, when more girls were wearing unisex clothes. Very, very slowly, everything became unisex, boys and girls were wearing jeans, boys and girls were wearing shirts, boys and girls were wearing pink. A lot of the women that I knew in the early days wanted to dress as men, which myself I can never understand because we weren't men, but that's the way they did it. But gradually it would be the black suits and the ties that were going out and the boys' names were going out. There were lots of Eddies around and Jacko and Scottie and names like that and then they stopped. I don't know any of them now that have got boys' names. But it was the unisex age, I think that meant that the lesbian didn't stand out as much. It was nothing to see a woman walking down the street in a pair of jeans and a shirt and people wouldn't have said, "Oh, lesbian," they would have looked and said, "I like your jeans." You know? It was a fashion thing. I've never discussed this with anybody, but on reflection I think it was that.

GILL:

I think there has been a general change in society's attitudes. When you think about the rights we've got now. We're not there yet, but some of the things, civil partnership, gay adoption, I didn't believe we would get. I think it's generational, it's not an issue so much, leaving aside homophobia in the playground and whatever. I think it's all part and parcel of that loosening up of attitudes. But then I can find myself thinking, "You've made all these changes," and then something happens and you think, "Oh God, we've still got such a long way to go." So I suppose it's about that feeling that you can't be complacent.

BOB L:

My fear is that if anything did happen, a really bad recession or something like that, the *Daily Mail* and all those would start another witch hunt against us and we'd be back where we started. That's what terrifies me.

STEPH:

I think younger lesbians feel that there isn't so much to fight for any more, they almost feel the battle has been won. I don't think it has, because I think society will only accept lesbians if they look attractive and normal, probably with long hair, probably a bit like on *The L Word*, they have to be attractive. All the lesbians they've had on soaps have always been like that, and if they're confronted with someone who definitely looks like quite a tough, butch woman, they're not so accepting at all. So I think there is still discrimination. I think there's still quite a long way to go before society accepts people who are different. I suppose the laws have made a difference; but they might have made a difference in what people can say but it can't alter what they think, and that is the thing.

SHARLEY:

I'm German by birth. One moment everything was lovely in Germany and the next people were dragged off into concentration camps. I was thirteen when I left Germany but I had to go back and I came to England again when I was sixteen, on the Kindertransport. I came to England just before the war. My father was murdered in a concentration camp and was beaten to death and my mother eventually died on transport to a concentration camp. My brothers and I got out.

So I suffer from an anxiety neurosis because I've experienced how quickly prejudices can be fed to rational human beings, because it's always easier to blame somebody.

I think people of colour will be the first to get it in the neck if that should happen, but I think they're probably strong enough to resist because of the numbers. But gays are an easy target, and having been at Speakers' Corner all these years, there's still a tremendous antagonism towards homosexuals.

SARAH:

I sometimes wonder if these young girls who openly walk about holding hands feeling very free, whether they realise what someone like Jackie Forster did, how she paved the way. It was a very difficult time in the 1950s.

RON:

We always had this thing, we said, "We're not going to be second-class citizens." Even then. Freedom isn't something that's given you forever and a day, you have to fight for it every day, and we had to bloody well fight.

After Oscar Wilde, it was all immoral and Satanic and whatever, and then to try and redress the situation, it had a medical label. I can remember reading this medical book when I was studying and it had a chapter about homosexuality and in this text book it said that you could tell gay men because they wore green carnations. This was a medical textbook! But in a way it was moving it away from the moral judgements.

BARBARA:

My generation could not even consider coming out. You were part of a life where you either had a simple job, perhaps secretarial or something and got married and everything was geared up towards the expectancy of that, or you had a career like teaching, which I did.

The first time I slept with a woman, I was twenty-one, and I think the lovely thing from that was I realised I was capable of enormous passionate love, and I'd always thought I was quite a chilly morsel before.

IRENE:

I used to put banners for the Pride march up on my vans and things and people used to say, "Oh you're not one of those, are you?" I turned round and said, "What do you mean, 'one of those'? Can you explain to me? What does 'one of those' mean? Are they different from you?" It's all: "It's not right. God doesn't make people like that, you shouldn't be like that." I said, "But it *is* like this. You've got to learn to live with it, you've got to learn to accept it." I say, "Because I'm a lesbian, every time you open the door, I'm not going to jump in bed with you, because it doesn't work like that."

I say: "The majority of lesbians, it's not because of sex, it's because you're enjoying female company, you understand each other, you have more communication, you have more gentleness and you care for one another. The sex is the last thing, companionship is more important. Companionship and affection and love, genuine love. That is why so many women like to be with other women, even the heterosexuals, they like to go out with the girls.

ROGER:
In the English language we only have one word for love and that is a disadvantage. Love means physical sex, plus an emotional relationship. The relationship I have with Ron now is not what I had in 1960. It was all hearts and flowers and birds singing. It's not like that now. It's like a comfortable slipper. We're not two people, we're one person.

JENNY:
I thought, "I cannot be the only person like me, there must be others out there. Perhaps it's just a matter of waiting until someone feels like I do – and I've got to be very careful." Because I knew it was very wrong.

I've always quite enjoyed dressing femme. Not really appearing at first glance, if you don't know about it, as obviously a lesbian. I like it to be a surprise to people. I don't like people to think 'dyke' the minute I walk in through the door, but maybe they do. It's just something you do, or what you give away, or just perfectly obvious. I don't know.

EMMANUEL:
I don't think I had any problem about being gay but I wanted it kept completely separate from the rest of my life. I had a life that was gay and a life that was not gay and never the twain shall meet.

GERARD:

There were no role models. Even the famous Julian and Sandy weren't really role models. They were caricatures. In books you were reading more about people having emotional feelings, but no role models. You didn't know anyone who was out and gay.

COLIN:

One of the things about the gay community is that it's enormously accepting. It takes people for who they are because what you have in common is a shared notion of being gay.

I think I'd always identified as gay even if I didn't actually have a gay identity, if you see what I mean. I always felt I was a bit different. I used to feel in my early twenties that I was totally on my own, that there was no other person like this in the world and yet I here I am, I've lived to tell the tale.

LEONARD:

Being gay is basically being a person... but it is special of course.

REFERENCES

Introduction

1 Personal Narrative Group (Eds). *'Truths', Interpreting Women's Lives: Feminist Theory and Personal Narratives*. Bloomington: Indiana University Press, 1989. 261. Print.
2 Postlewait, Thomas. *The Cambridge Introduction to Theatre Historiography*. Cambridge University Press, 2009. 251. Print.

Chapter 2: Once I Had a Secret Love

1 Weeks, Jeffrey. *The World We Have Won*. Oxon: Routledge, 2007. 49. Print.

Chapter 3: Being Illegal

1 Ireland, Doug. "Free the Buggers – Britain & the Wolfenden Report." *Gay City News*, 6 Sept 2007. Web. 2 May 2012. http://direland.typepad.com/direland/2007/09/index.html
2 Batten, Rex. *Rid England of this Plague*. London: Paradise Press, 2006. Print.
3 Ireland, Doug. "Free the Buggers." Op. cit.
4 Burton, Peter. *Parallel Lives*. London: GMP, 1985. 38. Print.
5 Pugh, Stephen. "The Forgotten." *Handbook of Lesbian and Gay Studies*. Eds. Diane Richardson and Steven Seidman. London: Sage, 2002. 166. Print.
6 Deveson, Anne. *Australians at Risk*. Sydney: Cassell, 1978. Print.
7 Uncovering Lesbian History Publications Group. "For Those Who Would Be Sisters: Uncovering Lesbian History." Birkbeck College, University of London, 1986. 38. Print.

Chapter 4: Coming Out and Going Out

1 Bridge, Haydon. "Old King Cole." *QX Magazine*. 24 Sept 2008. Web. 2 May 2012. http://www.qxmagazine.com/pdf/backissues/qx707.pdf

Chapter 5: The Shame of It All

1 Herek, Gregory M. "Facts About Homosexuality and Mental Health." Web. 2 May 2012. http://psychology.ucdavis.edu/rainbow/html/facts_mental_health.html

Chapter 6: Coming Together

1 Feather, Stuart. "A Brief History of the Gay Liberation Front, 1970–73." 21 Nov 2007. Web. 2 May 2012. http://libcom.org/library/brief-history-gay-liberation-front-1970-73

Chapter 7: Sapphic Lifelines

1 Pettitt, Ann. "No Failure Like Success." 18 Oct 2006. Web. 2 May 2012. http://www.opendemocracy.net/globalization-vision_reflections/greenham_4013.jsp
2 British Library. "Shrew." Web. 2 May 2012. http://www.bl.uk/learning/histcitizen/21cc/counterculture/liberation/shrew/shrew.html
3 London Feminist Network. "Why Reclaim the Night?" Web. 2 May 2012. http://londonfeministnetwork.org.uk/lfn-events/reclaim-the-night
4 Uncovering Lesbian History Publications Group. "For Those Who Would Be Sisters: Uncovering Lesbian History." Birkbeck College, University of London, 1986. 38. Print.
5 Rights of Women Lesbian Custody Group. *Lesbian Mother's Legal Handbook*. London: Women's Press, 1986. 121. Print.

Chapter 11: Classroom Closet

1 Herek, Gregory M. "Facts About Homosexuality and Child Molestation." Web. 2 May 2012. http://psychology.ucdavis.edu/rainbow/html/facts_molestation.html
2 Oram, Alison. "Embittered, Sexless or Homosexual: Attacks on Spinster Teachers 1918-39." *Not a Passing Phase*. Lesbian History Group. London: Women's Press, 1989. 99. Print.

Chapter 12: HIV/AIDS

1   Wellings, K. "Perceptions of Risk – Media Treatment of AIDS." *Social Aspects of AIDS.* Eds. P. Aggleton and H. Homans. Falmer Press, 1988. 87. Print. Cited in Avert. "History of AIDS up to 1986." Web. 2 May 2012. http://www.avert.org/aids-history-86.htm

2   Brunt, M. "Ban on Deadly Kiss of Life." *Sunday Mirror.* 17 Feb 1985. Cited in Avert. Op. cit.

3   Pinching, A. "Children with HIV Infection: Dealing with the Problem." *AIDS: A Challenge in Education.* Ed. D.R. Morgan. Institute of Biology, 1990. Cited in Avert. Op. cit.

4   UNAIDS. "Infographics." 23 Mar 2012. Web. 2 May 2012. http://www.unaids.org/en/resources/infographics

BIBLIOGRAPHY

Batten, Rex. *Rid England of this Plague*. London: Paradise Press, 2006.

Burton, Peter. *Parallel Lives*. London: GMP, 1985.

Cant, Bob, and Susan Hemmings. *Radical Records: Thirty Years of Lesbian and Gay History 1957–1987*. Abingdon: Routledge, 2010.

Duberman, Martin Bauml, Martha Vicinus and George Chauncey Jr, eds. *Hidden from History: Reclaiming the Gay and Lesbian Past*. New York: Meridian, 1990.

Faderman, Lillian. *Odd Girls and Twilight Lovers*. London: Penguin, 1992.

Faderman, Lillian. *Surpassing the Love of Men*. New York: William Morrow, 1981.

Gardiner, Jill. *From the Closet to the Screen: Women at the Gateways Club, 1945–85*. London: Pandora, 2003.

Hall Carpenter Archives Lesbian Oral History Group. *Inventing Ourselves: Lesbian Life Stories*. London: Routledge, 1989.

Hall Carpenter Archives Gay Men's Oral History Group. *Walking After Midnight: Gay Men's Life Stories*. London: Routledge, 1989.

hooks, bell. *Yearning: Race, Gender and Cultural Politics*. London: Turnaround, 1991.

Kaufman, Gershen, and Lev Raphael. *Coming Out of Shame*. New York: Doubleday, 1996.

Lapovsky Kennedy, Elizabeth, and Madeline Davis. *Boots of Leather, Slippers of Gold: The History of a Lesbian Community*. New York: Routledge, 1993.

Oram, Alison. "Embittered, Sexless or Homosexual: Attacks on Spinster Teachers 1918-39." *Not a Passing Phase*. Lesbian History Group. London: Women's Press, 1989.

Perks, Robert, and Alistair Thomson, eds. *The Oral History Reader*. London: Routledge. 1998.

Pugh, Stephen. "The Forgotten." *Handbook of Lesbian and Gay Studies*. Ed. Diane Richardson and Steven Seidman. Sage: London. 2002.

Rights of Women Lesbian Custody Group. *Lesbian Mother's Legal Handbook*. London: Women's Press, 1986.

Spargo, Tamsin. *Foucault and Queer Theory*. Cambridge: Icon Books, 1999.

Uncovering Lesbian History Publications Group. "For Those Who Would Be Sisters: Uncovering Lesbian History." Birkbeck College, University of London, 1986.

Weeks, Jeffrey. *The World We Have Won*. Abingdon: Routledge, 2007.

ABOUT THE AUTHOR

Clare Summerskill is a playwright, singer-songwriter, actress and lesbian comedienne. Clare regularly performs her own one-woman comedy shows and tours them to theatres internationally. She has written and produced several plays and films, mainly in the verbatim theatre style, made entirely from interviews and performed by members of her own theatre company, Artemis. These projects include: *Gateway to Heaven*, a play based on memories given by older lesbians and gay men; *Queens' Evidence*, a film about the relationship between the Metropolitan Police and older LGBT people; and *Hearing Voices*, a piece about the experiences of mental health service users, for which the script was published by Tollington Press in 2010. Her songs, stories and monologues are collected as *We're the Girls* (Diana Publishing 2008). Her short fiction also appears in *The Diva Book of Short Stories* (ed. Helen Sandler, Diva 2000), its sequel *Groundswell* (2002), and *Sinister Wisdom* (2011).